The Prophetic Quest

DIMYONOT דמיונות
Jews and the Cultural Imagination

Volumes in the Dimyonot series explore the intersections, and interstices, of Jewish experience and culture. These projects emerge from many disciplines—including art, history, language, literature, music, religion, philosophy, and cultural studies—and diverse chronological and geographical locations. Each volume, however, interrogates the multiple and evolving representations of Judaism and Jewishness, by both Jews and non-Jews, over time and place.

OTHER TITLES IN THE SERIES:

David Stern, Christoph Markschies, and Sarit Shalev-Eyni, eds., *The Monk's Haggadah: A Fifteenth-Century Illuminated Codex from the Monastery of Tegernsee, with a prologue by Friar Erhard von Pappenheim*

Ranen Omer-Sherman, *Imagining the Kibbutz: Visions of Utopia in Literature and Film*

Jordan D. Finkin, *An Inch or Two of Time: Time and Space in Jewish Modernisms*

Ilan Stavans and Marcelo Brodsky, *Once@9:53am: Terror in Buenos Aires*

Ben Schachter, *Image, Action, and Idea in Contemporary Jewish Art*

Heinrich Heine, *Hebrew Melodies*, trans. Stephen Mitchell and Jack Prelutsky, illus. Mark Podwal

Irene Eber, *Jews in China: Cultural Conversations, Changing Perspectives*

Jonathan K. Crane, ed., *Judaism, Race, and Ethics: Conversations and Questions*

Yael Halevi-Wise, *The Retrospective Imagination of A. B. Yehoshua*

Laura Levitt, *The Objects That Remain*

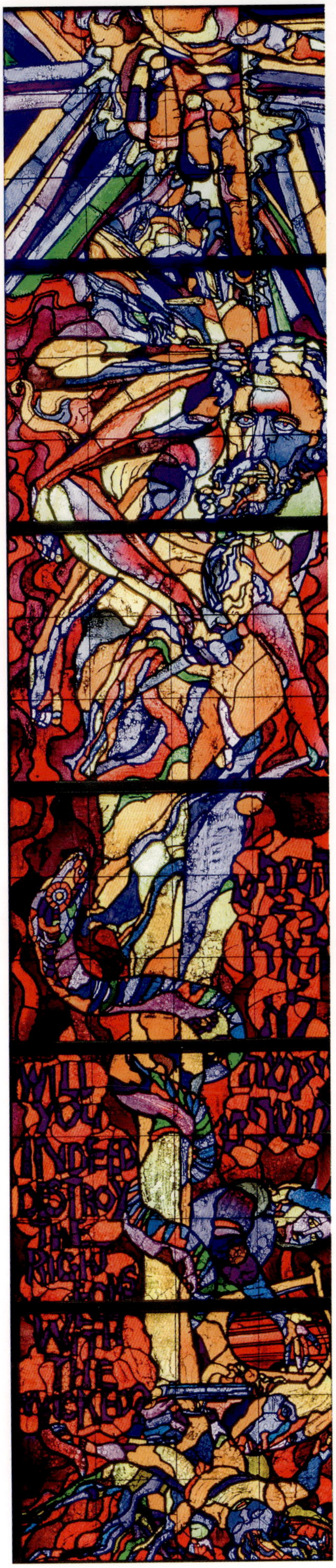

The Prophetic Quest

The Stained Glass Windows of Jacob Landau

REFORM CONGREGATION KENESETH ISRAEL, ELKINS PARK, PENNSYLVANIA

David S. Herrstrom
and Andrew D. Scrimgeour
with special contributors

Foreword by Thomas H. Kean
Photography by Tom Crane

The Pennsylvania State University Press
University Park, Pennsylvania

Library of Congress Cataloging-in-Publication Data

Names: Herrstrom, David Sten, 1946– author. | Scrimgeour, Andrew D., 1945– author.
Title: The prophetic quest : the stained glass windows of Jacob Landau, Reform Congregation Keneseth Israel, Elkins Park, Pennsylvania / David S. Herrstrom and Andrew D. Scrimgeour with special contributors ; foreword by Thomas H. Kean ; photography by Tom Crane.
Other titles: Dimyonot (University Park, Pa.)
Description: University Park, Pennsylvania : The Pennsylvania State University Press, [2021] | Series: Dimyonot: Jews and the cultural imagination | Includes bibliographical references and index.
Summary: "Explores ten monumental stained-glass windows, designed by the artist Jacob Landau, for the Keneseth Israel synagogue in Elkins Park, Pennsylvania"—Provided by publisher.
Identifiers: LCCN 2020040958 | ISBN 9780271087818 (cloth)
Subjects: LCSH: Landau, Jacob, 1917–2001—Criticism and interpretation. | Reform Congregation Keneseth Israel (Elkins Park, Pa.) | Stained glass windows—Pennsylvania—Elkins Park—History—20th century. | Jewish art and symbolism—Pennsylvania—Elkins Park—20th century. | Prophets in art.
Classification: LCC NK5398.L28 H47 2021 | DDC 748.509748/12—dc23
LC record available at https://lccn.loc.gov/2020040958

Printed in China
Published by The Pennsylvania State University Press, University Park, PA 16802–1003

The Pennsylvania State University Press is a member of the Association of University Presses.

It is the policy of The Pennsylvania State University Press to use acid-free paper. Publications on uncoated stock satisfy the minimum requirements of American National Standard for Information Sciences—Permanence of Paper for Printed Library Material, ANSI Z39.48–1992.

But I also say this: that light
is an invitation
to happiness,
and that happiness,

when it's done right,
is a kind of holiness,
palpable and redemptive.

—MARY OLIVER

Tell all the Truth but tell it slant—
Success in Circuit lies
Too bright for our infirm Delight
The Truth's superb surprise
As Lightning to the Children eased
With explanation kind
The Truth must dazzle gradually
Or every man be blind—

— EMILY DICKINSON

To

Constance Joy Herrstrom

prime mover of the
Jacob Landau legacy

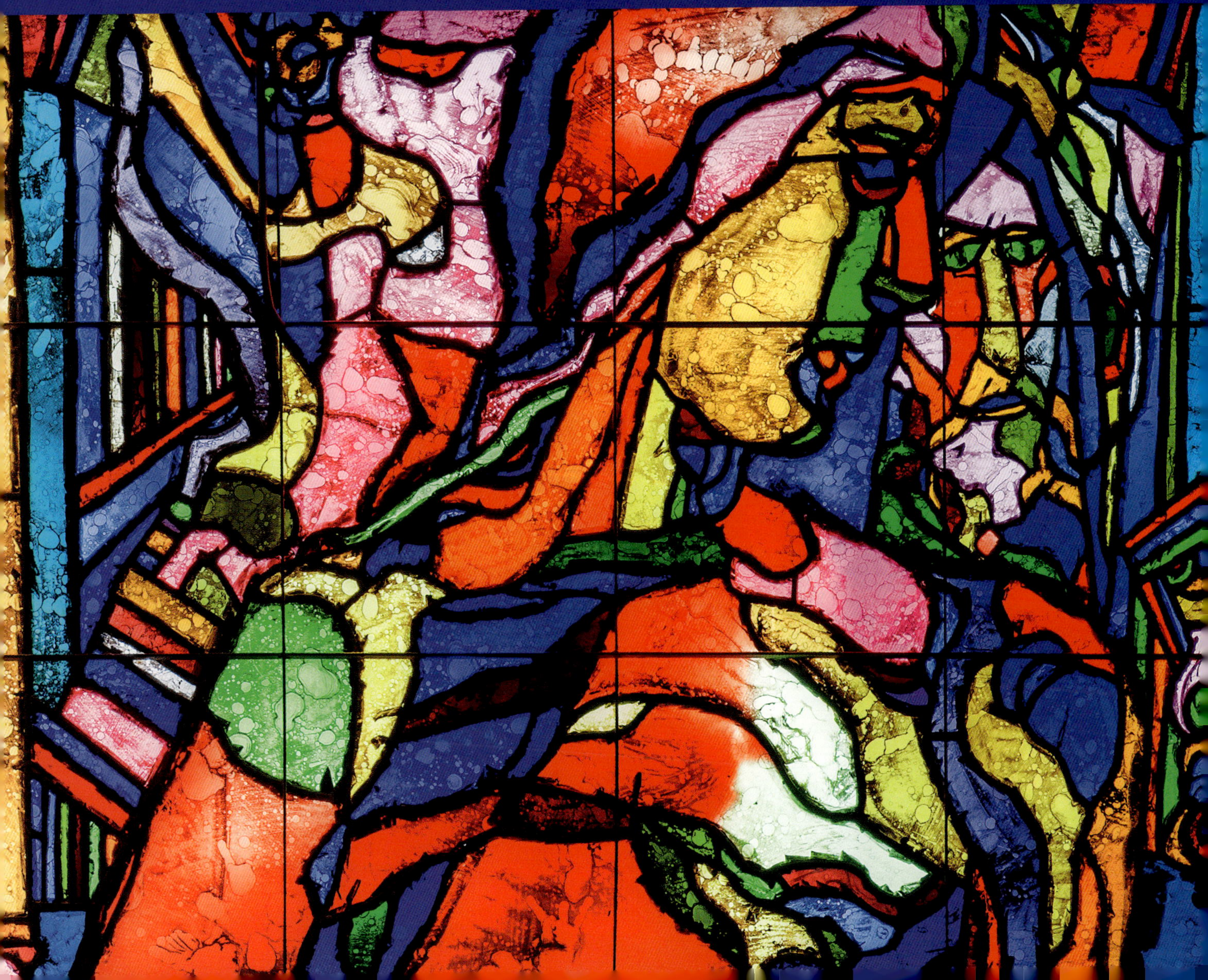

Contents

Essays

The Windows

Reflections

Illustrations

Foreword

Stained glass windows, whether in a house of worship or in a statehouse, always catch my eye. They tend to cast a spell, evoke a meditative mood, and inspire me to reaffirm the ideals they embody. Windows that interpret biblical texts are a particular favorite and go hand-in-hand with my love of illustrated Bibles. I have been collecting them for many years. Whether the artists are Gustave Doré, Marc Chagall, or Barry Moser, they bring fresh eyes to the text. The result is often striking, at times unsettling, always worth a linger.

I was pleased when the archives of Jacob Landau, one of New Jersey's finest artists, came to the Special Collections of the Drew University Library. While Landau illustrated many books, he never illustrated a Bible—at least not in the conventional way. Instead, he chose much larger pages—enormous panes of glass—on which to emblazon the life and passion of the ancient prophets.

When I first saw his soaring windows, especially their tangle of figures thrusting upward, I was reminded of the sculptures of Nathan Rapoport. Citizens of Philadelphia commissioned him to create the first public monument in North America to memorialize the Holocaust. It is located just a few miles south of the Landau windows in the center of downtown Philadelphia—the Monument to Six Million Jewish Martyrs.

Some years ago, I had the opportunity to talk with Rapoport about art and his terrible experiences during World War II. He said, "Art is for giving back. You take what you see, what you feel, your pain or joy. You make it into a gift, and you give it back to life."[1]

Now with this illuminating book by David Herrstrom and Andrew Scrimgeour, the audience for the windows will expand. Many more people will experience Landau's great gift.

THOMAS H. KEAN

GOVERNOR OF NEW JERSEY, 1982–1990

PRESIDENT, DREW UNIVERSITY, 1990–2005

Preface

Several years ago, 10,000 scholars of religion from the United States, Canada, and Europe converged in Philadelphia.[1] Complementing the lectures and scholarly papers were opportunities to visit works of art with religious themes that have captured the imagination of people from around the world, such as those in the Philadelphia Museum of Art, the Pennsylvania Academy of Fine Arts, the Woodmere Art Museum, and the synagogue designed by Frank Lloyd Wright.[2]

Less well known among these treasures was a group of stained glass windows that riveted the visitors, prompting the repeated response, "Why haven't we been aware of these before now? They should be known as a national treasure."

These ten monumental stained glass windows, designed by the nationally known artist Jacob Landau and titled *The Prophetic Quest*, declare their glory from the walls of the Reform Congregation Keneseth Israel in Elkins Park, a northern suburb of Philadelphia.

Towering twenty-five feet and blazing with color and light, each window is devoted to a biblical prophet. Images from their lives, rooted in their own time and re-imagined in ours, intertwine with biblical texts that proclaim the message of Abraham, Elijah, Amos, Hosea, Isaiah, Jeremiah, Ezekiel, Second Isaiah, Job, and Malachi.

As a curator at the Philadelphia Museum of Art observed, the windows "celebrate the lives of the prophets through color, rhythm, design, and majestic sweep."[3] At the same time, the bold colors and provocative designs of these windows are intended, like the prophets' words, to disturb. The call for justice in the world of human affairs is unmistakable.

Yet why weren't they better known? That question haunted us, prompting us to propose to the Jacob Landau Institute that we prepare a book for the general public—one that would convey the beauty of the windows and interpret their jarring iconography. They concurred.

This book is the result.

First and foremost, the book is designed to be a visual feast of the windows. Thanks to the artistry of Tom Crane, one of the country's leading architectural photographers, the ten windows can be viewed first all at once, in a panoramic sweep of the sanctuary; then a wave of five windows at a time on each side of the sanctuary; then each individually; then individual panels of some of the windows; and finally, details within several single panels.

The immersive visual experience of the windows is accompanied by four sections of text. The first section includes five essays that provide background and context for reading the windows: a biography of the artist, Jacob Landau; a history of the project;

the unique relationship of Landau with the stained glass specialist, Benoît Gilsoul; the perspective of the Senior Rabbi of the Reform Congregation Keneseth Israel, Dr. Lance Sussman; and finally, the vision that Landau himself had for the windows.

The second section is "Commentary." The biblical texts embedded in each window are identified and the Hebrew verses translated. All the figures and objects in the windows are identified and their location indicated. Finally, interpretive notes suggest the unsettling thrust of each window as Landau pursued his "prophetic quest."

The third section is titled "Reflections." We wanted to hear how a wide variety of people responded to the windows. So we invited artists, art historians, curators, biblical scholars, clergy, poets, and parishioners to write brief reflections on their experiences with the windows. The results were as varied as the images in the windows. Some are mini-essays, some are meditations, and others are poetic explorations. Each gives us new ways in which to see, as though for the first time, Landau's creation.

The book concludes with a number of helpful appendices: the technical specifications of the windows; an index to the images in the windows; an index to the biblical texts in the windows, including English translations of the Hebrew texts; a glossary of terms used in the text; a chronology of the life of Jacob Landau; and a bibliography of Landau's publications as well as literature on his life and work.

Our hope is that the volume enlarges the audience for the windows, deepens your understanding and appreciation of them, and inspires you to embrace the prophetic quest for justice.

D. S. H.

A. D. S.

Acknowledgments

On this book are the fingerprints of a host of talented and helpful people. We are in their debt.

Benefactors
- Michael and Noémi Neidorff

The Drew University Archives & Special Collections
- Matthew Beland, PhD
- Cassie Brand, PhD
- Brian Shetler, PhD

Monmouth University
- Scott Knauer

Reform Congregation Keneseth Israel and Temple Judea Museum
- Norman Brody
- Jack Myers
- Rita Rosen Poley
- Brian Rissinger
- Pam Saltzburg
- Senior Rabbi Lance Sussman, PhD

Duke University Divinity School Library
- Rebecca Bowers

Archivists and Librarians from
- Marquand Art Library, Princeton University
- North Carolina State University Libraries (D. H. Hill Jr. Library and James B. Hunt Jr. Library), Raleigh
- Harry Ransom Humanities Research Library, University of Texas, Austin
- Pratt Institute, Brooklyn, New York
- University of Oregon, Eugene
- Eva Perry Regional Library, Apex, North Carolina

Penn State University Press
- Patrick Alexander
- Laura Reed-Morrisson
- Kathryn Yahner
- Brian Beer

Jacob Landau Institute Board
- Rosa T. Giletti
- Jill Grieveson
- Constance J. Herrstrom (consultant)
- Rebecca Mebert
- Saliba Sarsar, PhD
- Rod Tulloss, PhD (former member)

As well as
- Ana Debevec
- Jean Farnsworth
- Tristen Herrstrom
- Peggi Howard
- Hannah Kaufman
- Jeff Mantler
- James Preis
- Dorothy Scrimgeour
- Meghan Scrimgeour, PhD
- R. Blair Stiefbold
- Aaron Woolsey

The Prophetic Quest

Essays

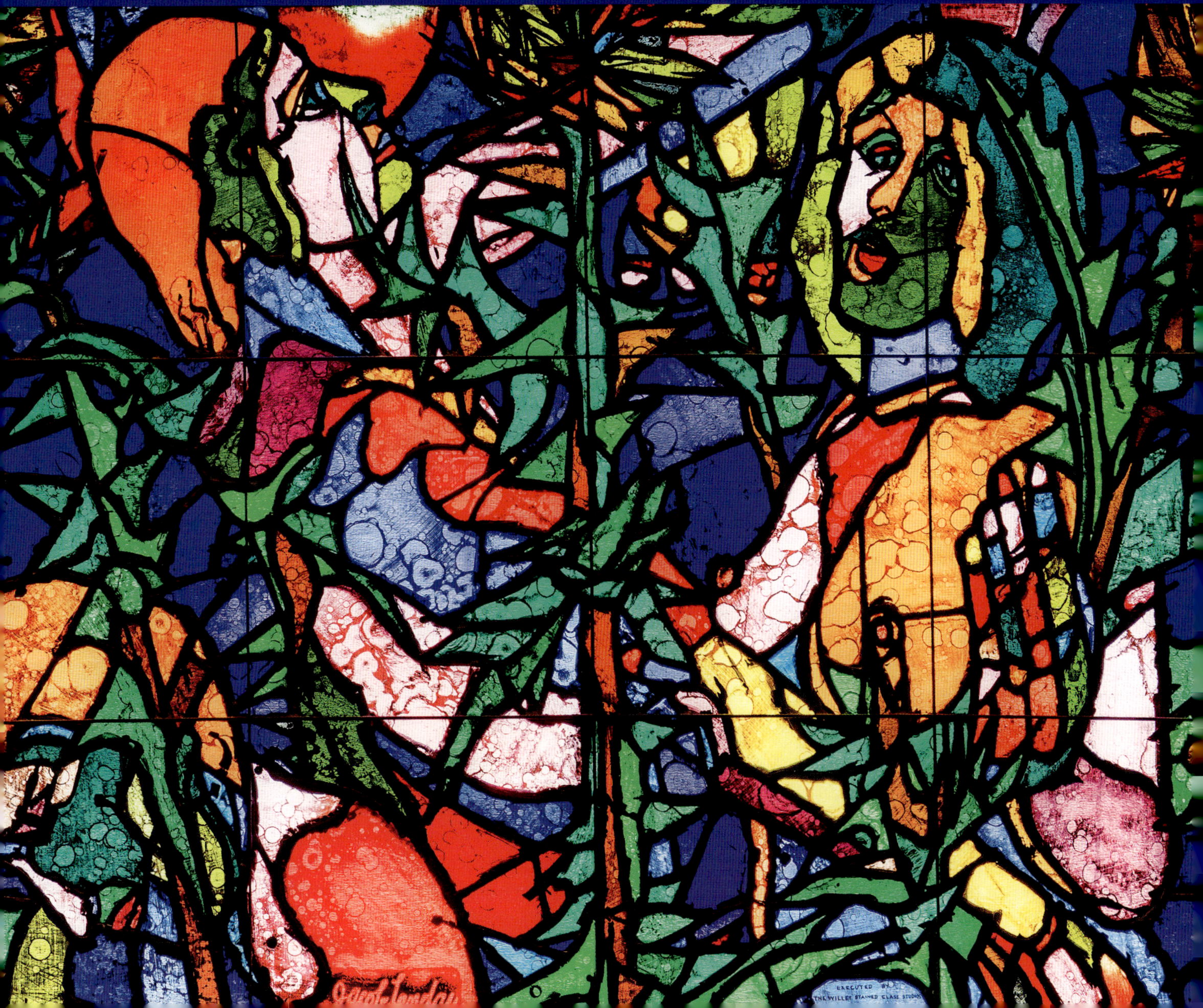

Prophet with a Brush

The Life of Jacob Landau

Andrew D. Scrimgeour

Few artists can claim to have won a national art competition and captured the attention of the press while still in their teens. Jacob Landau can make that boast, and his victory included an unusual bonus—a one-person show that toured the country with stops in San Francisco, Chicago, Boston, and New York.

For almost a century, Scholastic, publisher of classroom newspapers for middle and high school students, has conducted an annual competition—the prestigious Scholastic Art and Writing Awards—to discover and honor highly talented teenagers.[1] While a student at Overbrook High School in Philadelphia, Landau won top honors in Scholastic's graphic arts competition. And not just once, but two years in a row.[2] Only four other students have achieved that two-time distinction. (Even Andy Warhol, another Pennsylvanian who won the art competition ten years later, is not a member of that elite group.[3]) But before Landau's first award was finalized (1934), an astounded but wary jury felt compelled to telegraph Landau's principal and ask him to certify that the portfolio Jacob had submitted was truly his own work. In their judgment, his brush-and-ink illustrations for Kipling's *Jungle Book* were too exquisite for even the most advanced teenager. Upon announcing the second award a year later (1935), Scholastic packed up Landau's portfolio of fifty-eight animal sketches for a cross-continental tour.

Landau's early maturation as an artist was hardly a fluke. Born on December 17, 1917, in Philadelphia, he grew up in a family, a public school system, and a city that valued the arts and knew how to nurture young talent. His father, an immigrant from Warsaw, Poland, was a painter in the Cubist tradition and a poet.[4] Jacob's first professional group exhibition found him and his father appearing together in the 128th Annual Exhibition at the National Academy of Design in New York.[5]

But his father's studio was not where it dawned on Jacob that the world of paint and palette could be more than a splendid hobby. That happened at school, in the sixth grade. As the Great Depression deepened and art supplies became precious commodities, his principal gave him a coveted bottle of Higgins India ink for his sole use.[6] That

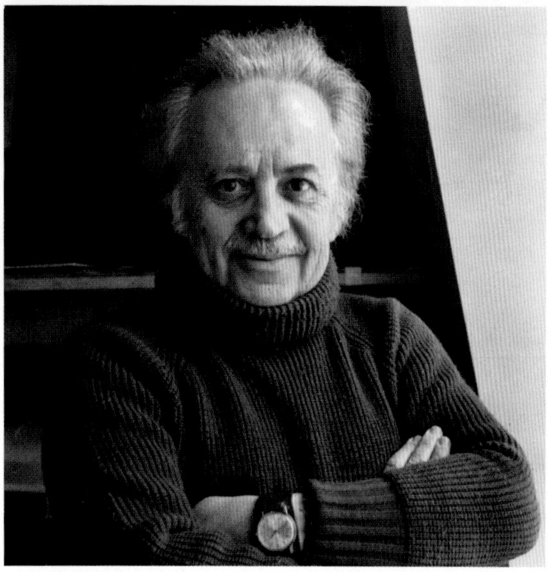

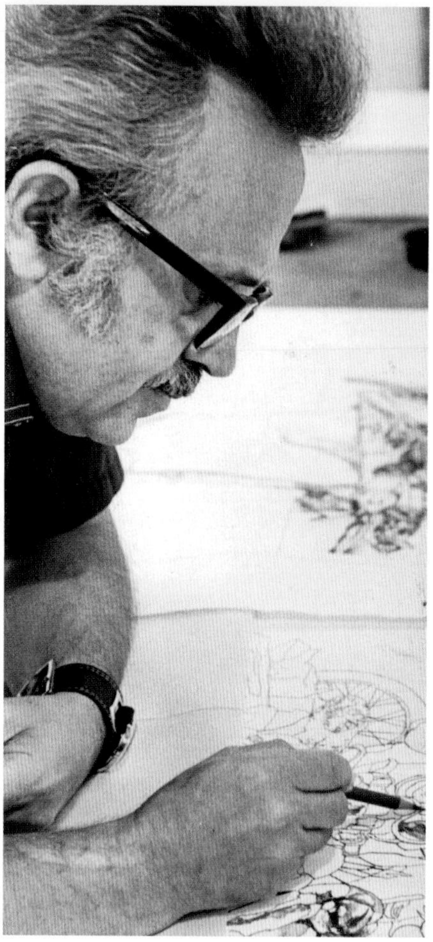

LEFT Jacob Landau. From the private collection of Rosa T. Giletti.

RIGHT Jacob Landau at work in his studio. With permission of the Archives of Reform Congregation Keneseth Israel and Temple Judea Museum, Elkins Park, Pennsylvania.

affirmation of his ability from a respected authority outside the family was akin to an anointing. It awakened in Jacob the realization that he was seen not as a dilettante but as a budding artist, and he began to take on that role with great seriousness.[7] He devoted every spare moment to drawing, and he ranged over the city on his bicycle, a bespectacled, eagle-eyed detective looking for subjects to capture in his sketchbook.[8] The Philadelphia Zoo and nearby Fairmount Park were rewarding territories for investigation, as were the docks on the Schuylkill River and the doorways of downtown buildings that harbored the homeless.[9]

Whenever Jacob could, he headed to the epicenter of art in Philadelphia—palatial Memorial Hall in Fairmount Park, the predecessor to the Philadelphia Museum of Art and a durable symbol of Philadelphia's long embrace of the arts.[10] He did not linger in the ornate rooms of European masterworks or along the corridor of medieval stained glass panels.[11] On most occasions, his destination was an exhibit room on the lower level, where he peered through porthole windows, each no larger than a soup bowl, to take in a riveting diorama—the destruction of Pompeii. Transfixed, he could not take his eyes off the anguished tangle of human figures fleeing the fiery flood of Mount Vesuvius. Those scenes scorched his soul and haunted him for the rest of his life.[12]

Because Landau had earned national attention as a precocious artist and had graduated at the head of his high school class, he won a scholarship to the Philadelphia Museum School of Industrial Art, located in the Memorial Hall that he already knew so well.[13] During his college days and three years beyond, he studied with artists who not only enjoyed national reputations for their work but also took pride in teaching the crafts of illustration, etching, drawing, painting, and printmaking—Earl Horter, Henry C. Pitz, Franklin Watkins, and Benton Spruance, among others. Even World War II and the long arm of the draft board did not derail his artistic progress. During the final two years of the war, he was stationed with the Army in Naples, Italy, and served as the art editor, photographer, and reporter of *At Ease*, a Special Services magazine.

With the help of the GI Bill, he resumed his formal studies at the New School for Social Research, where he met Leonard Baskin, artist and founder of the renowned Gehenna Press, which published finely illustrated books. Later, Baskin shared a house in Paris with Landau and his young family, and he introduced Landau to the art of the woodcut. Landau's three years in Paris were crowned by his first one-person show, a series of woodcuts and lithographs, at Galerie Paul Lebar (1952). Not only did the show win critical acclaim, but many of the artists Landau most admired purchased prints for their own collections.[14]

When Landau returned to New York with his wife and two young sons, he knew it was time to change his "artist in a garret" approach to living. While illustrating books and LP record jackets, he also discovered what proved to be long-term financial security—mentoring college students. He began teaching studio arts part-time at his old alma mater, now renamed the Philadelphia College of Art. Three years later, he was invited to join the faculty of the Pratt Institute in Brooklyn, where he achieved tenure.[15] Classes in drawing, printmaking, and illustration were his forte, and he gained a reputation as a master teacher. Recalling his early forays into Philadelphia neighborhoods, pad and pencil in hand, he said, "Art education must make the student into an active forager, a shaper of meaning and purpose, rather than a passive recipient."[16] For almost thirty years, he commuted three times a week to the Brooklyn campus from his home in central New Jersey, reserving the other days for work in his own studio.

Landau had moved to Roosevelt, a small town in rural New Jersey, in 1955 at the invitation of Ben Shahn, a nationally known artist who was dedicated to the New Deal and the relief of those suffering under the Great Depression. He and Shahn had become friends in New York. Both men, along with Baskin, valued art as a tool for social transformation. They also pursued figurative art despite the dominance of the abstract expressionist movement that had captured the art world.[17] The opportunity to have such a friend as both neighbor and interlocutor—and to live in the country—made Roosevelt irresistibly attractive for Landau. He was able not only to purchase a house but also to build an additional room for his first real studio. The days of cramped quarters in tiny loft apartments, with the kitchen table doubling as an art space, were over.

Landau flourished in Roosevelt. The village was an enclave of artists, many of whom were Jewish immigrants from Europe. Originally founded as an agro-industrial cooperative under the New Deal, it initially housed two hundred garment workers, formerly employed in New York City sweatshops, and their families.[18] Landau lived

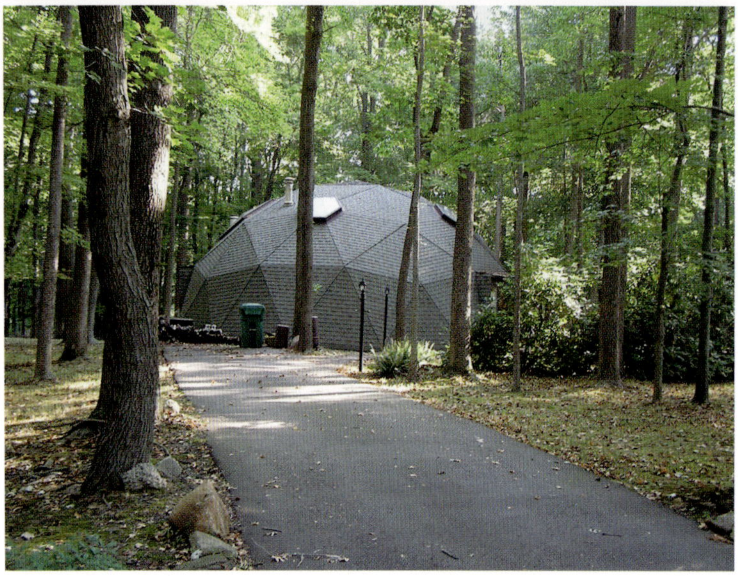

Jacob Landau's studio, Roosevelt, New Jersey. Photo: R. Blair Stiefhold.

there for the rest of his life. The move to Roosevelt was not only good for his art but good for his health as well. He had developed an allergy to oil paints and solvents. With the encouragement of Shahn, his neighbor, he switched to watercolors and was thrilled with the endless variations of color he could create. A few years later, in 1963, he won the coveted Philadelphia Watercolor Prize at the Pennsylvania Academy of Fine Arts Annual Show.

Landau became known in town as the artist with the most distinctive studio. In 1975 he built a geodesic dome as his studio, which was a ten-minute walk from his house. It was designed by his friend Buckminster Fuller and constructed by a company located in Roosevelt. This dome, suffused with light—with its two-story great room, an abundance of plants, the music of Beethoven's piano sonatas playing, and Lustau deluxe cream sherry waiting in the cupboard—became his haven.

To explore the breadth of Landau's artistry over the decades, whether by thumbing through his catalogue raisonné or by walking through an exhibit of his work, is to be struck with at least three undeniable impressions. First, the intricacy of the designs. The compositions are complex, asking to be read. The eye cannot take everything in, and you return to them again and again and find new elements, as though the works were alive and generating new elements as a tease. Second, the human body is everywhere. Landau was obsessed with the human body. The sinewy agony from the Philadelphia Vesuvius dioramas was never far from his consciousness. For him the human figure was not only an object but also "a symbol expressive of our common predicament, of the beauty and horror of existence. . . . It is paradigmatic of the human condition . . . every emotion, trait, and fate can be conveyed through the body."[19] It is the locus of great joy and of great suffering. His gauge of the moral integrity of a society or group of people throughout history was how people in power treated the bodies of the powerless.

Finally, Landau's canvases are not pretty. The colors are always dazzling but the paintings, woodcuts, and illustrations as a whole make the viewer uncomfortable.

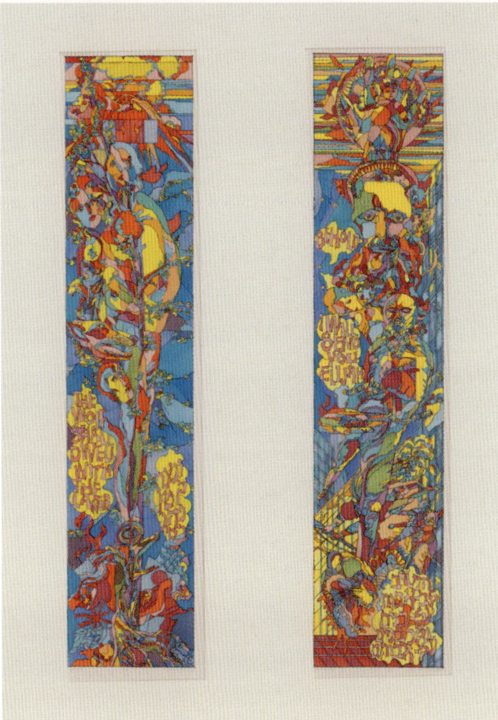

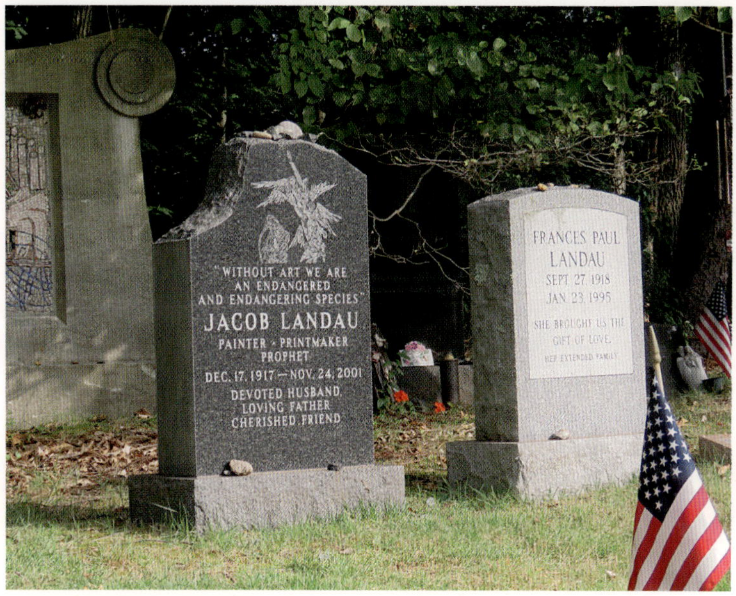

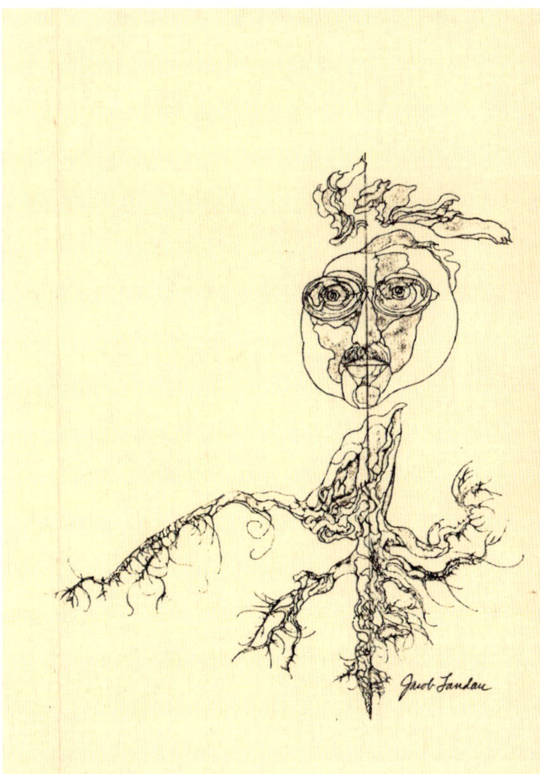

CLOCKWISE FROM TOP LEFT

Jacob Landau, watercolors (pochoir) of Isaiah and Malachi. Jacob Landau Collection, Monmouth University Galleries. Courtesy of Monmouth University.

Gravestones of Jacob and Frances Landau. Photo courtesy of Tristen Herrstrom.

Jacob Landau, self-portrait and autograph. From the private collection of David Herrstrom.

A humanist, Landau insisted that art must do more than entertain or please; it must join hands with "the tradition of protest that comes from the prophets of the Old Testament. They were concerned with justice and injustice."[20] They were angry, but hopeful, too. So was Landau. As one poet wrote, his art would have us soar "with prophets leading away / from stumbling, dark pits, and / satanic wheels / toward the New Jerusalem."[21]

After the death of his wife and the waning of his own energies, Landau became increasingly concerned with end-of-life issues, especially his finances and the disposition of his art. Would his art endure? He became alarmed when a friend of his, a local artist, died and his family hurriedly divested themselves of his work, tossing the art into dumpsters, oblivious to their value or his legacy. Consequently, Landau's representative, Rosa Giletti, assumed a larger role, aggressively placing his art in major museums and university collections and arranging shows across the country. Later, she became the executrix of his estate.

He also asked for advice from a certified financial planner, Constance Herrstrom, a neighbor, whose practice was in Princeton. Their client relationship had already been established several years earlier. In exploring the options for his estate and financial affairs, she proposed a framework that put the responsibility for his art and legacy into the hands of trusted friends, so that after Landau's death there would be time to ensure his legacy. He agreed, and several years later, the Jacob Landau Institute was born. Subsequently, the Institute entered into agreements with Drew University and Monmouth University for the permanent care of his papers and works of art. Unlike many artists, he gained the satisfaction that his life's work would be valued in perpetuity.

After a long struggle with Parkinson's disease, Landau died on November 24, 2001. He was 83, the same age his father was when he died. Located on the brow of a small hill at the edge of the Roosevelt cemetery and standing next to the tall memorial of his friend Ben Shahn, Landau's black granite tombstone is readily identifiable. Etched in its surface are the words "Jacob Landau—Painter, Printmaker, Prophet." Above the letters rises an exultant angel, as if in flight, its arm uplifted—a drawing by Landau.[22] Yet his signature words below add tension to this final canvas: "Without art we are an endangered and endangering species."[23] Armed with words and images, the artist presses his prophetic claims, even in death.

The Windows
Conception and Chronology

Andrew D. Scrimgeour

To walk into the sanctuary of Keneseth Israel is to enter a serene and awe-inspiring space, one where visitors speak quietly and move instinctively up the aisles to get a better view of the majestic windows that grace the walls—stained glass windows creating a stunning avenue of color leading to the ark.

But it was not always so. For seventeen years the room resembled a handsome auditorium more than an uplifting place of worship. The ark, bimah, and ner tamid (eternal flame) were in place, but the room lacked warmth and aesthetic distinction. Ten towering windows dominated the walls, five to a side, but they were milky white and absolutely opaque—blank placeholders conveying the unmistakable message that the sun-deprived room was still under construction.[1]

In 1957, when Keneseth Israel (KI) moved from Broad Street in central Philadelphia to a new campus in suburban Elkins Park, the congregation did not have the funds to commission the stained glass windows they envisioned for the new sanctuary. As had been the tradition in their former synagogues, they wanted distinctive works of art to illumine their worship space and were content to wait until that could be accomplished without compromise.[2]

While fundraising for the windows began almost as soon as the congregation moved to Elkins Park, planning for the actual windows remained on hold for thirteen years. Momentum for the project grew gradually as families in the congregation learned that the windows offered a distinctive and lasting way to create a memorial for a family member or esteemed friend. In early 1970, Senior Rabbi Bertram W. Korn announced that funding for four of the ten windows was committed and more were under discussion. Formal planning could begin.[3] A Stained Glass Windows Committee was formed, and Korn determined that it would be a lay committee; neither he nor any of the clergy would be members.[4] Ruth Schwerin, who had a background in art and was a collector of stained glass, and Bernard Bloomfield, a collector of decorative arts, were named the cochairs of the committee.[5] Their responsibility was twofold:

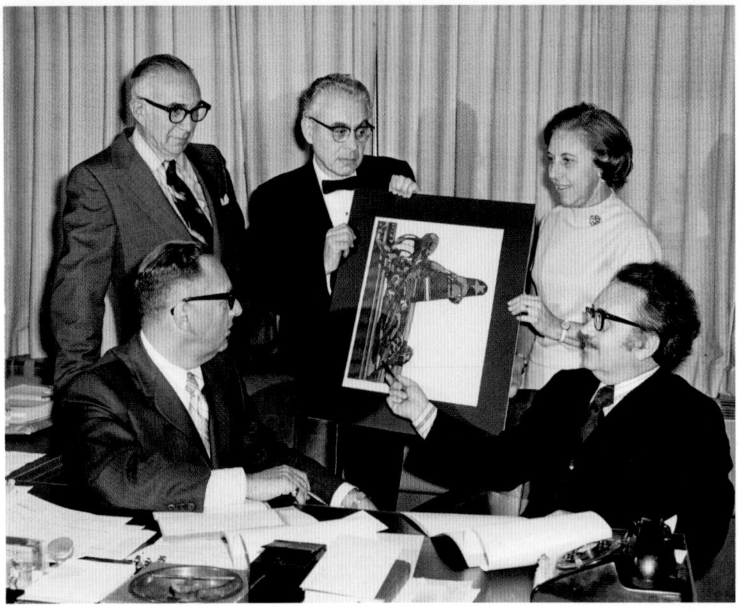

Members of KI Stained Glass Windows Committee with Rabbi Korn: (*standing, left to right*) Bernard Bloomfield, Co-Chairman; Dr. Rabbi Korn; Mrs. Louis Schwerin, Co-Chairman; (*seated*) Louis Schwerin, President of Congregation; and Jacob Landau. With permission of the Archives of Reform Congregation Keneseth Israel and Temple Judea Museum, Elkins Park, Pennsylvania.

selecting an artist to design the windows and choosing a firm to manufacture and install them. Their recommendations would go to the board of trustees for final action.

Early in its work, the committee reached consensus on six fundamental issues:

1. The windows would reflect a single unifying theme.
2. Abstract designs would be favored over realistic ones.
3. Faceted glass that allowed the spaces between the glass segments to vary would be preferred over the standard leaded glass option.
4. High-quality external lighting was essential to ensure the radiance of the windows during the Friday Shabbat liturgy and other evening services.
5. Artists who had not achieved fame would be considered along with those who had—that is, local artists would be on an equal footing with those who enjoyed national acclaim.
6. The artists did not need to have had prior experience with stained glass.[6]

The committee created a list of candidates consisting of three Jewish artists: Abraham Rattner, Chaim Gross, and Jacob Landau. (Marc Chagall, who created dreamlike images floating in stained glass, was unavailable.)[7] All three worked in varying styles of abstract art. Rattner was the only one of the trio who had actually completed a commission in stained glass. Both Rattner and Gross had, like Shahn and Chagall, created large-scale windows—a technical benchmark not insignificant to the KI project. Architectural critic Brian de Breffny, upon seeing Rattner's dramatic three-story stained glass wall in the sanctuary of the Chicago Loop Synagogue, said that it was "perhaps the most beautiful synagogue interior in the United States."[8] Congregations across North America vied with one another for Rattner's designs. Chaim Gross, on the other hand, was a sculptor best known for his large-scale works in bronze; he had studied at the Pennsylvania Academy of Fine Arts and was a friend of Rattner and Ben

LEFT Cover of *Out of the Whirlwind*.

RIGHT Cover of *Ramparts* magazine.

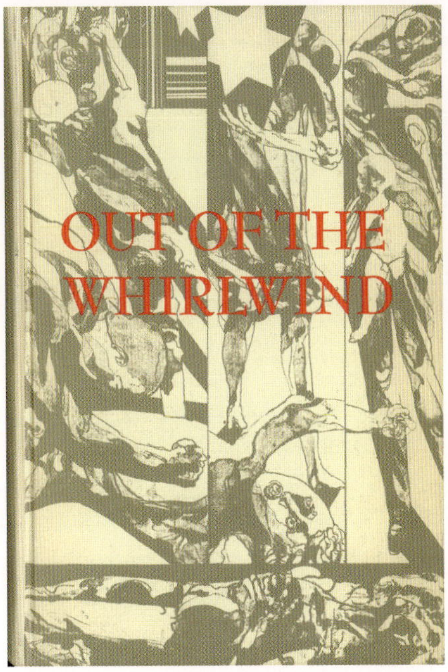

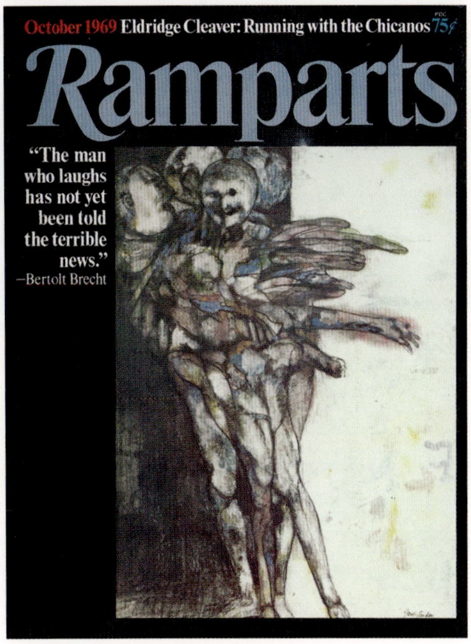

Shahn, a leading artist of social protest. Some have speculated that Shahn, Landau's well-known friend and neighbor in Roosevelt, New Jersey, would have been on the short list, too, but he died the year before the committee began its work.[9]

While Landau did not enjoy the renown of the other two artists, many members of the KI congregation were already familiar with his work. A much-discussed book at the time, *Out of the Whirlwind: A Reader of Holocaust Literature*, featured cover art by Landau and included the riveting lithographs of his *Holocaust Suite*. Edited by Albert H. Friedlander, an influential rabbi in the Reform movement, the book had been published two years before and was prominent in bookstores across the country, including the bookstore at KI.[10] Readers of the influential magazine *Ramparts* also knew Landau.[11] In October 1969, his work appeared on its cover and throughout the issue. It was the first and only time in the magazine's history that a single artist was given that honor.

Landau was a social critic and humanist. His art vividly exposed the cruelty of humans against humans—the death camps of Poland, the killing fields of Vietnam and Cambodia, and the assassinations in Dallas and Memphis. The committee chose Landau in part because of his concern with social justice.

The contract for the project stipulated that Landau would prepare preliminary sketches for the ten windows and submit them to the committee and the board of trustees within six months. The board would then decide whether to accept them and proceed with the project or terminate the contract and turn to other artists.

The biblical prophets caught Landau's imagination for the KI project. "I wanted to do the prophets almost immediately," he said, "because they represent the best elements in Judaism, in that they essentially were protesters and rebels and people who were inclined to uphold morality and ethical behavior."[12] He studied the ancient texts and consulted major commentaries, including the works of Abraham Heschel, Martin Buber, and Karl Jung. But it was Buber's *The Prophetic Faith* that became his

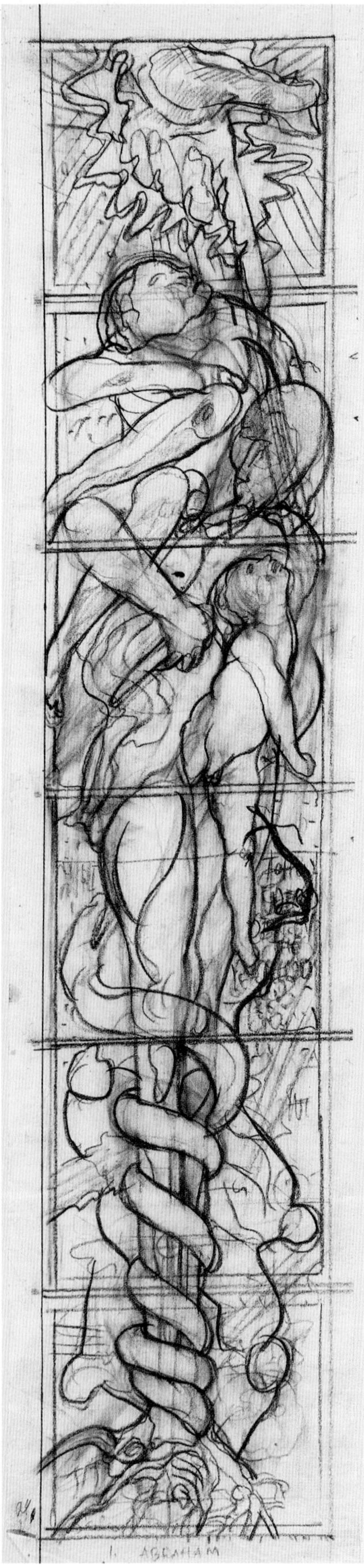

primary tutor. Contrary to a persistent misunderstanding, the biblical prophet (*nabi*), in Buber's view, "was no clairvoyant but the bearer of a 'word' of God that he spoke as an alternative placed before the people in a concrete situation."[13] He was not foretelling the future; he sought to change the inequities of the present. The prophets insisted that there can be no division between the "religious" and the "social." To be the people of Yahweh, they thundered, requires a revision of the social order—one that takes the side of the oppressed.[14] As Jon Levenson notes, "Unlike so many scholars of the Hebrew Bible, Buber does not get lost in the details of compositional, religious, or political history, nor does he hyper-focus on the exegesis of particular verses. Rather, his attention lies on what is most important to him . . . the personally and socially transformative encounter with the eternal You."[15]

Landau had never attempted a project of this size and complexity, and he found that developing the concepts and the sketches required more time than was allotted in the contract. Almost a year later, he presented sketches for what he called a "cycle of windows" with the theme "The Prophetic Succession," with "Good and Evil" a subtheme. Their function was to "detail the essence of the prophetic mission and experience. . . . Between God and suffering a mysterious connection exists, pointing the way to purification."[16] Each window portrayed a biblical prophet, the cycle beginning with Abraham and ending with Malachi.

The sketches and one finished painting for the windows generated excitement and vigorous discussion. Two of the donors had seen the sketches and registered their approval, as had four art experts, including the dean of the Tyler School of Art at Temple University. When the final vote was taken by the board of trustees, it was an overwhelming affirmation: twenty-one to seven. The committee was commended for fulfilling its charge. The concerns of the minority voices were not unexpected—unhappiness with the "busyness" of the designs, worry that the color palette was too complex to be fully captured in glass, and discomfort with the images of stark atrocities that would be permanently lodged in the sanctuary.[17]

As Landau refined the drawings, he met with the committee, the rabbinic staff, and the board for what were always spirited discussions. Some worried about the size and ferocity of the lion in the top panel of the Amos window, the sadness in so many of the faces, and the depiction of a revolver in the Abraham window. Equally fascinating are the questions that apparently were not raised. Why not a window to Deborah, the woman prophet?[18] Where were the ravens or the widow of Zarephath in the Elijah window, or the mountaintop temple of Isaiah?[19] And

OPPOSITE Jacob Landau, sketch of the Abraham window. Woodmere Art Museum: Gift of Rosa T. Giletti, 2015. Courtesy of the Woodmere Art Museum.

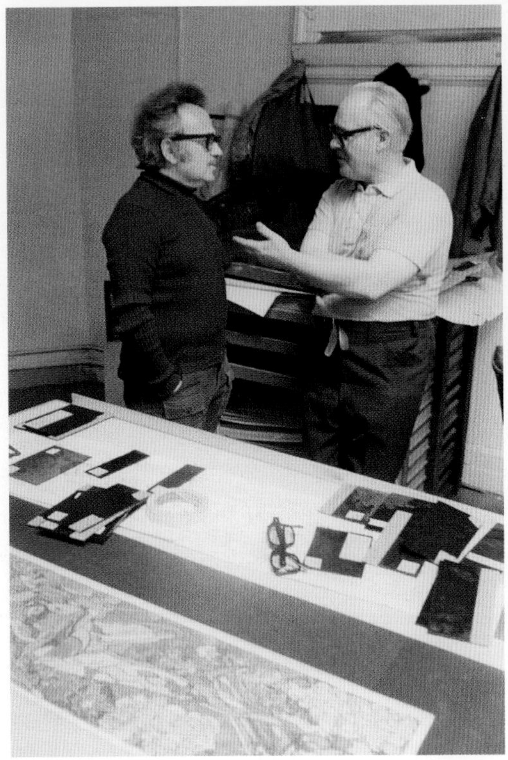

RIGHT Benoît D. Gilsoul with Jacob Landau. With permission of the Archives of Reform Congregation Keneseth Israel and Temple Judea Museum, Elkins Park, Pennsylvania.

why not a window for Moses, Judaism's supreme prophet?[20] While Landau protected his independence as an artist, he was sensitive to the suggestions and concerns of the committee members and the clergy and made changes to the drafts as his work progressed.

The project brought technical challenges. How could Landau's intricate watercolor drawings (the size of a large jigsaw puzzle or poster) be faithfully translated to monumental cartoons measuring five by twenty-five feet (the actual size of each window)? Could appropriate glass be found to capture Landau's subtle ranges of color? Not having worked with stained glass before, Landau needed the assistance of experienced artists.

Fortunately, Willet Stained Glass Studios, one of the oldest and largest companies in North America specializing in the design, fabrication, installing, and restoring of stained glass windows, was located in Philadelphia. Among its famed commissions were the Great Sanctuary Window for the Cadet Chapel at the United States Military Academy at West Point and windows for the National Cathedral in Washington, DC, and the United Nations in New York. Willet had also recently completed the installation of two of Ben Shahn's windows.[21] The committee chose the Willet Studios for the KI project.

Working for the studio was one of the finest stained glass artists in the world, Belgium-born Benoît D. Gilsoul. He had recently worked with Ben Shahn to translate his paintings for the leaded glass windows at Temple Beth Zion in Buffalo, New York.[22] Landau undoubtedly knew of him through Shahn and, like Shahn, had the utmost confidence in him, praising him for his technical prowess and sensitivity to his work.[23] A unique partnership evolved, its success owing to Gilsoul's attitude. As he said, "I

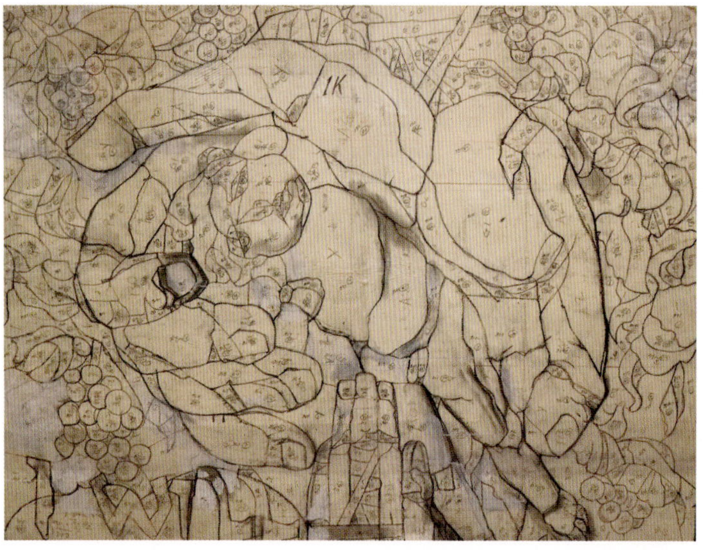

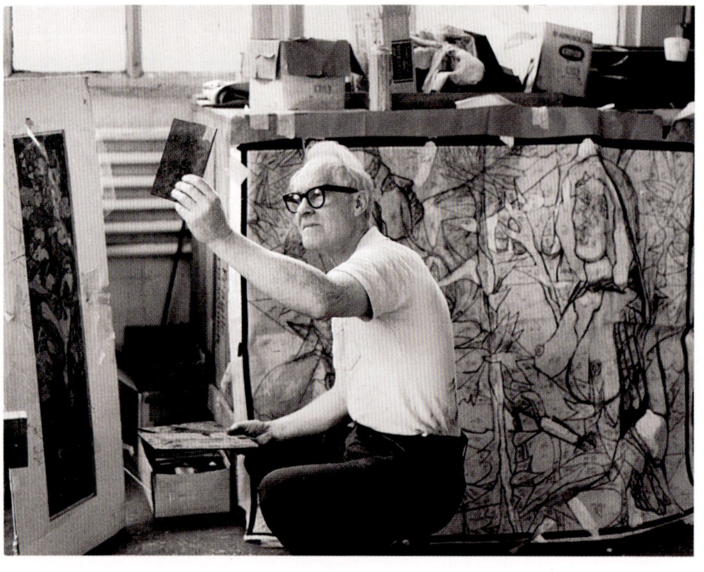

TOP Window cartoon for Hosea (panel 1). With permission of the Archives of Reform Congregation Keneseth Israel and Temple Judea Museum, Elkins Park, Pennsylvania. Photo: Marlene Adler.

BOTTOM Benoît D. Gilsoul matching colors with preliminary window cartoon behind him. With permission of the Archives of Reform Congregation Keneseth Israel and Temple Judea Museum, Elkins Park, Pennsylvania.

tried to understand the best I could [Landau's] philosophy, his way of doing work, and I processed and visualized this very well so that we could work together peacefully and in good spirits."[24]

Gilsoul searched for stained glass colors to match Landau's paintings as closely as possible. He chose hand-blown glass from North America and Europe, sometimes laminating pieces, sometimes painting them with mixtures of powdered metallic oxides and ground glass to gain texture and shadings of color. In the end, one hundred different colors were used. The sky outside the sanctuary would provide additional ever-changing subtleties to the palette. Gilsoul also translated the drawings into the large window-size cartoons from which Willet craftsmen cut the individual pieces of glass—some three thousand pieces for each window—and then joined them.

GATEFOLD *The Prophetic Quest*, Keneseth Israel Synagogue sanctuary, Elkins Park, Pennsylvania. First wave of windows, from back to front, on the left: Abraham to Isaiah; second wave, from back to front, on the right: Jeremiah to Malachi. Photo © 2013 Tom Crane Photography.

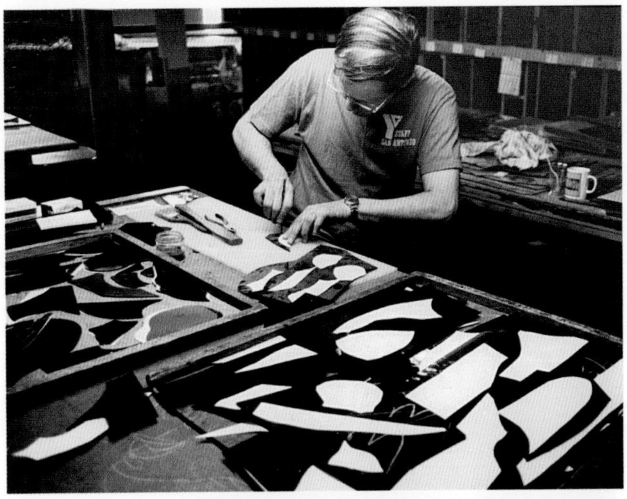

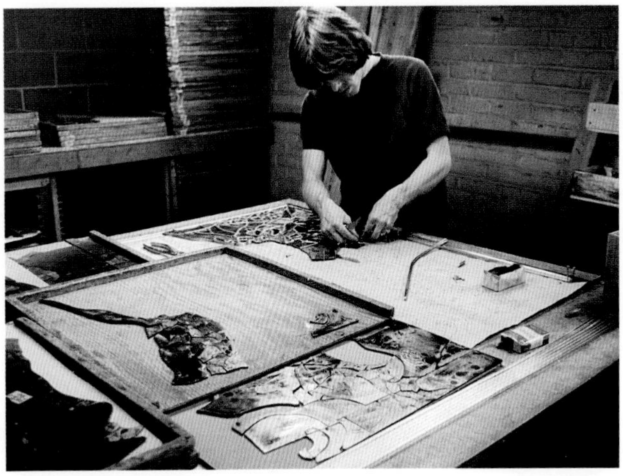

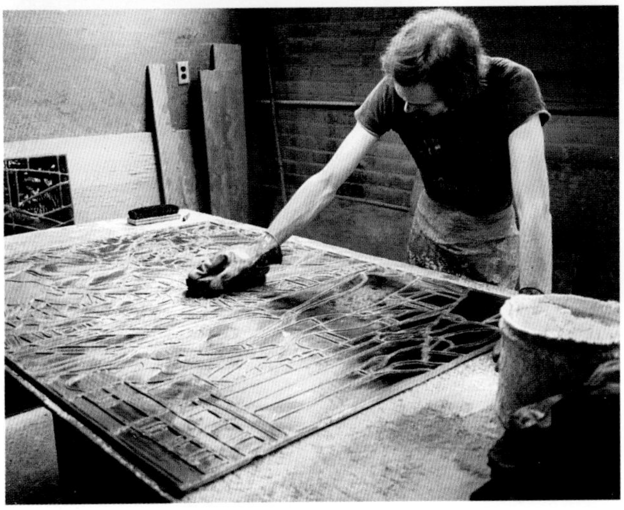

CLOCKWISE FROM TOP LEFT

Craftsman at Willet Studios cutting glass. With permission of the Archives of Reform Congregation Keneseth Israel and Temple Judea Museum, Elkins Park, Pennsylvania.

Craftsman at Willet Studios leading and soldering glass. With permission of the Archives of Reform Congregation Keneseth Israel and Temple Judea Museum, Elkins Park, Pennsylvania.

Craftsman at Willet Studios sealing glass after leading. With permission of the Archives of Reform Congregation Keneseth Israel and Temple Judea Museum, Elkins Park, Pennsylvania.

For the first time, Willet combined two joining techniques for the extraordinarily large number of tiny curved elements: the traditional lead method—characteristic of most stained glass windows since the twelfth and thirteenth centuries—and the soldered copper foil technique, seen in Tiffany glass, in order to give definition and strength where needed.[25]

Even as Willet proceeded with the installation, an essential part of the project was still missing: a name for the windows. Their concept was clear, but it had not crystallized into a succinct phrase. For Landau, the naming of his art could sometimes take a long time; selecting a title was part of the final "transformation of the image."[26] Just before the last window was installed, the name became clear to him: *The Prophetic Quest*.

When the windows were presented to the public, Kneeland McNulty, curator of prints at the Philadelphia Museum of Art, wrote, "The translation of Landau's original drawings into stained glass is an extraordinary achievement that may well mark a significant moment in ecclesiastical art."[27] A host of others—the KI congregation, art

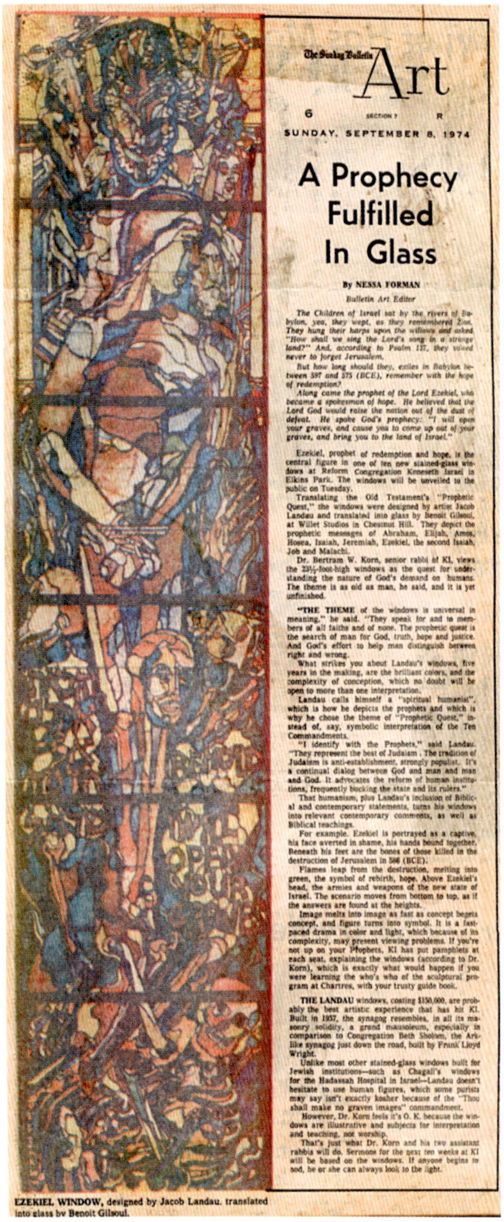

The Sunday Bulletin **Art**

6 SECTION 7 R

SUNDAY, SEPTEMBER 8, 1974

A Prophecy Fulfilled In Glass

By NESSA FORMAN

Bulletin Art Editor

The Children of Israel sat by the rivers of Babylon, yea, they wept, as they remembered Zion. They hung their harps upon the willows and asked "How shall we sing the Lord's song in a strange land?" And, according to Psalm 137, they vowed never to forget Jerusalem.

But how long should they, exiles in Babylon between 597 and 575 (BCE), remember with the hope of redemption?

Along came the prophet of the Lord Ezekiel, who became a spokesman of hope. He believed that the Lord God would raise the nation out of the dust of defeat. He spoke God's prophecy: "I will open your graves, and cause you to come up out of your graves, and bring you to the land of Israel."

Ezekiel, prophet of redemption and hope, is the central figure in one of ten new stained-glass windows at Reform Congregation Keneseth Israel in Elkins Park. The windows will be unveiled to the public on Tuesday.

Translating the Old Testament's "Prophetic Quest," the windows were designed by artist Jacob Landau and translated into glass by Benoit Gilsoul, at Willet Studios in Chestnut Hill. They depict the prophetic messages of Abraham, Elijah, Amos, Hosea, Isaiah, Jeremiah, Ezekiel, the second Isaiah, Job and Malachi.

Dr. Bertram W. Korn, senior rabbi of KI, views the 23½-foot-high windows as the quest for understanding the nature of God's demand on humans. The theme is as old as man, he said, and it is yet unfinished.

"THE THEME of the windows is universal in meaning," he said. "They speak for and to members of all faiths and of none. The prophetic quest is the search of man for God, truth, hope and justice. And God's effort to help man distinguish between right and wrong.

What strikes you about Landau's windows, five years in the making, are the brilliant colors, and the complexity of conception, which no doubt will be open to more than one interpretation.

Landau calls himself a "spiritual humanist", which is how he depicts the prophets and which is why he chose the theme of "Prophetic Quest," instead of, say, symbolic interpretation of the Ten Commandments.

"I identify with the Prophets," said Landau. "They represent the best of Judaism. The tradition of Judaism is anti-establishment, strongly populist. It's a continual dialog between God and man and man and God. It advocates the reform of human institutions, frequently bucking the state and its rulers."

That humanism, plus Landau's inclusion of Biblical and contemporary statements, turns his windows into relevant contemporary comments, as well as Biblical teachings.

For example, Ezekiel is portrayed as a captive, his face averted in shame, his hands bound together. Beneath his feet are the bones of those killed in the destruction of Jerusalem in 586 (BCE).

Flames leap from the destruction, melting into green, the symbol of rebirth, hope. Above Ezekiel's head, the armies and weapons of the new state of Israel. The scenario moves from bottom to top, as if the answers are found at the heights.

Image melts into image as fast as concept begets concept, and figure turns into symbol. It is a fast-paced drama in color and light, which because of its complexity, may present viewing problems. If you're not up on your Prophets, KI has put pamphlets at each seat, explaining the windows (according to Dr. Korn), which is exactly what would happen if you were learning the who's who of the sculptural program at Chartres, with your trusty guide book.

THE LANDAU windows, costing $150,000, are probably the best artistic experience that has hit KI. Built in 1957, the synagog resembles, in all its masonry solidity, a grand mausoleum, especially in comparison to Congregation Beth Sholom, the Ark-like synagog just down the road, built by Frank Lloyd Wright.

Unlike most other stained-glass windows built for Jewish institutions—such as Chagall's windows for the Hadassah Hospital in Israel—Landau doesn't hesitate to use human figures, which some purists may say isn't exactly kosher because of the "Thou shall make no graven images" commandment.

However, Dr. Korn feels it's O.K. because the windows are illustrative and subjects for interpretation and teaching, not worship.

That's just what Dr. Korn and his two assistant rabbis will do. Sermons for the next ten weeks at KI will be based on the windows. If anyone begins to nod, he or she can always look to the light.

EZEKIEL WINDOW, designed by Jacob Landau, translated into glass by Benoit Gilsoul.

Newspaper headline on the completion of the KI windows: Nessa Forman, "A Prophecy Fulfilled in Glass," *Sunday Bulletin*, September 8, 1974. With permission of the Archives of Reform Congregation Keneseth Israel and Temple Judea Museum, Elkins Park, Pennsylvania.

critics, journalists, and visitors across the country—joined in that affirmation. Keneseth Israel had achieved its long-sought goal: creating a sun-saturated treasure for its sanctuary—one that bathed the congregation in beauty while reminding them that the quest for justice is the supreme act of worship.[28]

The Unexpected Provenance of *The Prophetic Quest*

Rita Rosen Poley

As a museum curator, I have long been fascinated by the provenance, or history, of an object. Regarding Jacob Landau's *The Prophetic Quest* the facts are well known. We know who commissioned the work, who created it, when, where, and even why. But there is another layer of understanding—another, more subtle, type of "provenance"—that can enhance our appreciation of this extraordinary achievement in the art of stained glass.

The Willet Studios, Jacob Landau, and Benoît Gilsoul, the major players in the creation and fabrication of these ten massive windows, each brought a unique history to *The Prophetic Quest*. In studying each separately I began to sense a certain synergy that was never a stated criterion of the search for artist or fabricator.

In the mid- to late 1950s, Henry Lee Willet, an active member of the Stained Glass Association of America (SGAA), served as one of the lead organizers for a unique project. In cooperation with the American Federation of Art, the association sponsored a number of well-received exhibitions in which artists who had never worked with stained glass were invited to submit designs for a work in glass. SGAA member studios executed the accepted designs, and the project resulted in the development of new fabricating techniques, expanded markets, and more artists in the mix of contemporary glass. Abraham Rattner, who was later considered for the Keneseth Israel commission, was one of these artists and was subsequently launched as a respected stained glass artist. Widespread press coverage included headlines such as "Revival in Glass" and "Stained Glass Has Graduated from the Gothic."[1]

This openness of Willet Studios toward working with artists unfamiliar with stained glass continued when Benoît Gilsoul (1914–2000) came to work for them in 1963. Little is known about the Belgian-born Gilsoul's experience of working in stained glass before coming to the United States in 1960 at the age of forty-six. A precocious artist from a very young age, by 1933 he had already founded the Sécessionist art group L'Esquisse, an influential group of young Belgian artists. In 1935, while still a student at the Académie Royale des Beaux-Arts, the top Belgian art college, he collaborated in the design for the Pavillon de la Vie Catholique at the Brussels World's Fair. By 1958 he had had fifty one-man shows. In 1960 he secured the sponsorship of New York glass artist Jean-Jacques Duval and was able to come to the United States. In Duval's studio, he developed his passion and talent for the art of stained glass. In 1963, as a mature glass artist, he came to Willet Studios.

On the occasion of Gilsoul's seventy-fifth birthday celebration, E. Crosby Willet, Henry's son, said, "Benoît Gilsoul arrived at the Willet Studios in Chestnut Hill on [*sic*] January, 1963, and from that date until he left for New York to open his own studio, he was one of the finest artists ever associated with our group in its ninety-one year history."[2] At Willet, a firm that described itself as early as 1921 as "an organization of artists, designers, and craftsmen in ecclesiastical and domestic art"—thus putting the "artist" first—Gilsoul truly was at home. "He not only designed . . . projects, but was a major influence in their exquisite execution in both the selection of glass and the painting of the glass."[3]

In 1967 he worked with Ben Shahn (1898–1969) on a Willet project for Temple Beth Zion in Buffalo, New York: a massive nonobjective glass wall, *God Speaking to Job from the Whirlwind*. Shahn had never worked with stained glass, and it was the responsibility of Willet and Gilsoul to translate one of his paintings, purchased earlier by the congregation, into a work of glass art. Gilsoul and Willet successfully brought their own artistic understanding of material and technique to a "conversation" that bridged the aesthetic, the religious, and the technical. A few years later they would take this collaborative approach a giant step further with Jacob Landau, who also had never previously worked with stained glass. With Shahn's work, Gilsoul's challenge—to introduce the medium of light into the translation of a design originally conceived to exist only on paper—must not be underestimated. But Gilsoul's love affair with the action of light on glass is readily apparent in the legacy of his work. As he said, "It lives with light graciously lent to us and with light no lie is possible."[4]

Equally apparent, in his own words, is Landau's relief at finding that, with Gilsoul, he was in the hands of an artist who spoke his language: "He understood immediately what I had in mind. His extraordinary sensitivity to the character of my line and my use of color enabled him to approach perfection as an interpreter."[5] The importance of this understanding cannot be overstated. Gilsoul's project at Temple Beth Zion involved the execution of an existing work by Ben Shahn. *The Prophetic Quest*, in contrast, was an original commission, and the collaboration between Gilsoul and Landau was essential to the success of the project.

So in this search for the unexpected "provenance" of *The Prophetic Quest* we have traced the willingness of Willet Studios to work with artists inexperienced with stained glass. We have seen that even Benoît Gilsoul—one of the most noted stained glass artists and technicians of his time—came later to the profession with a solid traditional background in the fine arts that perhaps enhanced his comfort level in interpreting works by non-glass artists. And surely with Jacob Landau's strong commitment to narrative art, a hallmark of most religious stained glass, the collaboration with Willet and Gilsoul was a comfortable prospect.

But what about the synagogue? Why did the members of Keneseth Israel choose an artist who had never worked in stained glass to fulfill such a massive project? Certainly the extent of the work—ten windows, each over twenty-five feet high and over five feet wide, with a surface of three thousand square feet—might have given them pause. And there was also the matter of style. In 1970, when the synagogue awarded the contract to Landau, abstract expressionism had been the dominant mode of American art for almost two decades. Even the 1967 Shahn window at Temple Beth Zion is pure abstraction.

However, in 1962, the Museum of Modern Art held a landmark juried show, *Recent Painting USA: The Figure*, which traveled to six other major museums. Included in the show was a work by Jacob Landau, one of 74 works chosen by Alfred H. Barr Jr., director of museum collections, from nearly 9,500 entries. As Judith Stein observed, "The existence of a major exhibition of figurative art at the Museum of Modern Art was national news. *Time* magazine ran a well-illustrated story on 'the reappearing figure.'"[6] Landau was, according to *Time*, "brave enough to admit being concerned with 'the condition of man.'"[7]

At the time he received the KI commission, Landau had a stellar reputation, with his work exhibited and collected by museums internationally. Beyond his fame, and equally germane to an understanding of KI in its choice of Landau, was the fact that "Jacob Landau [was] always attracted to the Bible as a source of narrative," as Stein put it. She added, "biblical archetypes provided him with both literal subject and covert content," and he "remained committed to the delineation of the human body."[8]

Indeed, throughout his entire oeuvre, and especially in *The Prophetic Quest*, we see Landau's fundamental passion saying, "I am interested in art as advocacy of the human, as revelation of the tragic, as hope of transcendence."[9]

So I throw into the mix—risk-takers all—the artistry and humanist vision of Jacob Landau, the creativity of Willet Studios, and Benoît Gilsoul, who returned to Willet in order to work with Landau to interpret his vision and execute his massive masterpiece. First and foremost, *The Prophetic Quest* is a work of art. Yes, it has a profound message, and surely it is that message, along with the experienced talents of Willet and Gilsoul, that propelled Keneseth Israel to "follow the art" and have the confidence to embark on its own prophetic quest.

In Situ

A View of the Landau Windows from the Pulpit of Reform Congregation Keneseth Israel

Lance J. Sussman

During the job interview that brought me to the pulpit of Reform Congregation Keneseth Israel in Elkins Park, Pennsylvania, one of the themes I constantly heard from congregational representatives was "the windows." "You have to see the windows at the end of Yom Kippur," I was regularly told. "They are beautiful."

Sure enough, at the end of my first High Holy Day season in 2001, the sunlight came pouring through the Landau windows in the KI sanctuary, transforming the entire room into a golden, sacred space. It was indeed beautiful and, biblically speaking, "awesome"!

However, my first experience of the windows on Yom Kippur also awoke a different, more complex emotion in me. There was something wrong in the congregants' reports about the beauty of the windows. Were the windows really meant to be beautiful? Were the prophets beautiful? Is the prophetic quest a beautiful message or is it something else? As a religious studies major at Franklin and Marshall College and then again as a rabbinic and graduate student at the Hebrew Union College–Jewish Institute of Religion (Cincinnati), I had been taught that the prophets were challenging, troubling, disturbing, and unsettling; they were the epitome of good preaching both "afflicting the comfortable and comforting the afflicted." Maybe from a lofty, metaphysical point of view they were "beautiful," but not in any normal aesthetic sense of the word.

I began to wonder if my congregants' views of the windows were beside the point. Were they confusing the ornamental aspect of the windows with their deeper message, seeing the windows as the historical completion of their sanctuary (built in 1957 with frosted windows), a monumental beautification project and not a set of provocative, upsetting, and teleologically inspiring statements by the artist-prophet Jacob Landau?

Naturally, given my own background as a rabbi and a historian, I decided to learn more about Landau himself and the window project. It immediately became clear to me that there was more to the windows than a sanctuary art project. I knew the prophets had a message. The question became, What was Landau's message? A second question for me was, How did synagogue leadership and the senior rabbi, Bertram W. Korn, understand that message? Ultimately, how did the windows reflect the theology of American Reform Judaism in the early 1970s?

After approximately two years of research, I began to form my conclusions about the worldview of the Landau windows, and they were startling. First, the windows are essentially secular and humanistic, and not inherently religious. Second, with respect to Reform Judaism they are a historical bookend, almost anachronistic, in their treatment of prophetic Judaism. Third, they are a modernist heresy and codify critical biblical theory. Fourth, they are bibliocentric and barely refer to the rabbinic tradition. Fifth, they are uninfluenced by Heschel's landmark *The Prophets* (1962), the most important late twentieth-century Jewish interpretation of ancient Israel's prophets. And finally, in both American and Jewish ways, they ultimately affirm the idea of progress and reaffirm a belief in hope for the future. In short, their historical specificity as a 1970s statement about Reform Judaism, not their lucent afternoon colors, became my primary way of relating to them.

My first order of business was to research the life and art of Jacob Landau. Although born Jewish, Landau did not demonstrate any interest in Jewish themes in his art until 1968, when he illustrated the cover of Albert H. Friedlander's *Out of the Whirlwind: A Reader of Holocaust Literature* for the press of the Reform movement in Judaism. By contrast, his friend, neighbor, and colleague Ben Shahn, who was of an equally humanist bent, had been recruited by the American Jewish community fourteen years earlier, when it celebrated its tercentenary in 1954. When Keneseth Israel failed to recruit Marc Chagall to its stained glass window project, it turned to Landau, conveniently located in nearby Roosevelt, New Jersey, and a partnership was forged.

The theme agreed upon for the project was anything but avant-garde or daring. Although Keneseth Israel had distinguished itself during the American Civil War as an abolitionist congregation, it subsequently became known for its anti-Zionism and largely sat out the tumultuous years of the civil rights movement and the Vietnam War. In addition to his work at the synagogue, Rabbi Korn, who served Keneseth Israel from 1949 to 1979, was a rear admiral in the United States Navy and eschewed the protest movements of the day. A theological liberal, he neither challenged Reform Judaism as "Prophetic Judaism" nor embraced the "death of God" theology of some of his more radical colleagues. By the early 1970s, it was broadly accepted that Reform Judaism was slipping into a kind of malaise, no longer tightly connected to its past self-definition as Jewish ethical monotheism and not yet redefined by a mix of neo-traditionalism and feminism.

To ground himself in the literature of the Hebrew prophets, Landau surprisingly turned to Martin Buber and his classic 1949 study, *The Prophetic Faith*. Buber, who generally held more sway among Christian theologians than Jewish thinkers, seeks to recover the existential reality of the prophets and their dialogical encounter with the God of Israel. By contrast, for the more fully humanistic Landau, identifying prophetic themes and tying them to contemporaneous issues was paramount. For Buber, the prophets represented God's quest to confront ancient Israel in a specific time and place. For Landau, the prophets' quest was to confront us in our time and our place.

In many ways, the downward-turned hand at the top of the Abraham window is the most important image in the Landau windows. To Landau, justice, the ultimate prophetic quest, is essentially a human quest, not a divinely commanded goal. Anticipating a later pivot in the book of Job, the windows are not about questioning God but about trying to discover the highest human aspirations. Like Buber, Landau remained a Hebrew humanist and embraced the challenges of the prophets both for ancient Israel and for humanity in modern times. In so doing, he made the window project his own "prophetic quest," perhaps memorialized in the fusion of his own face with that of the prophet Malachi in the final window.

The most accessible image in the Landau windows, in my experience, is found in the bottom panel of the Amos window. In it, Landau depicts a modern band playing so loudly that "we" cannot hear the prophet's urgent message. One of the band members is shown holding a green electric guitar. Invariably, I begin my tours of the windows by asking new viewers, especially younger visitors, to find that guitar. As soon as they find it, the imagery of the windows opens for them. I quickly redirect them to the top of the window and the large image of the lion roaring out the prophet's message of justice. At this point, depending on the age of the visitors, I may tell them about how the synagogue's board objected to the ferocity of Landau's lion and insisted he make it smaller. I can only imagine the artist cringing in his effort to compromise with synagogue leadership.

In other windows, Landau clearly pushed the envelope with synagogue leadership. Jewish ceremonial art is highly respectful of the principle of *tzniut*, or modesty. Not so Landau. In both the Hosea and Jeremiah windows, there is male and female nudity—breasts and a penis are displayed following the biblical texts. In this regard, the artist follows the prophets in challenging everyday sensibilities and smashes social convention with impunity.

The bottom of the Isaiah window contains a second artistic challenge to conservative social convention. To illustrate the discord among nations, Landau selected the flags of various nations, including the Soviet Union and "Red" China. Imagine, in the waning days of the Vietnam War, a synagogue agreeing to display in perpetuity the flags of America's communist enemies! Equally sensational for Keneseth Israel was the decision to embed the Israeli flag in the same display. At the time, only the American flag was displayed in the KI sanctuary, a silent echo of the congregation's pre-1948 anti-Jewish statehood views. In fact, an actual Israeli flag was not installed in the sanctuary until 2002. The other muted references to Israel in the windows are the weapons being held upward at the top of the Ezekiel window, which, despite its depiction of the Valley of Dry Bones, is not explicit in terms of a Holocaust reference.

Viewing the Landau windows in situ necessitates comment on the ark in the KI sanctuary. Depicting the life of Moses in gild, the panels were fabricated in 1938 for the synagogue's previous temple on North Broad Street at Columbia in North Philadelphia. Originally designed to stand alone, the panels now can be seen as part of a broader statement about the supremacy of the prophecy of Moses in the Jewish tradition. Moreover, Landau chose gold to represent the divine in his windows at Keneseth Israel. The combination of the ark and windows in the sanctuary is seamless and powerful.

The last window, Malachi, is a statement about the future and is boldly modern in its depiction of great skyscrapers. It speaks to a kind of faith in progress, untempered by the disasters of the twentieth century, and echoes the concluding passage of the Hebrew Bible that the ultimate source of peace is domestic tranquility. The window, like the prophet, merges the personal and the societal with ease, leaving the viewer in awe of the project's majesty and filled with hope.

Finally, a word about what is *not* in the Landau windows. Had he worked on the same project even five years later, it is hard to imagine that Landau would not have included at least one of Israel's female prophets. Buber in particular pays a great deal of attention to the prophet Deborah. Also missing from the windows are any significant references to rabbinic Judaism or Jewish mysticism. Of course the late twentieth-century neo-traditionalism of the Reform movement was just beginning to assert itself in the early 1970s. However, in their fullness and complexity, the windows created by Landau are powerful, not only because they are spectacular and beautiful, but also because they are truly prophetic. They speak truth in defiance of social convention. They affirm. They challenge. They inspire and, in the golden light of a Yom Kippur afternoon, they sanctify.

The Prophetic Quest of Jacob Landau

David S. Herrstrom

Blazing colors, sensuous lines, and the sheer grandeur and authority of these monumental windows stun us. On first encounter, they move some to tears; others, to rapture. For none are they a serene experience. Seductive rhythms transport us; sharp, initially baffling images unsettle us. We simply cannot view these windows as we would decorative paintings on a church or temple wall. Their overwhelming emotion, focused by a steely intelligence, invites confrontation. Their majestic sweep casts a spell, yet questions us, causing a shiver of unease because we want to enter the artist's images and at the same time back away from their fire. We are witness to something truly new in the thousand-year-old tradition of spiritual expression in stained glass.

The richness of *The Prophetic Quest* did not appear in a sudden vision but was the culmination of a long struggle. The curve of Landau's life and career reveals the importance of these ten stained glass windows to the artist and the man. The commission to create Keneseth Israel's windows seemed to Landau a dream project.[1] It was not only a challenge, at a collaborative and architectural scale he had never before attempted, but it was far beyond an ordinary work, being monumental public art in an unfamiliar medium—stained glass. It would not be hidden away in a private living room. Moreover, Landau was given complete freedom to choose his subject and develop his images, reserving the right as an artist to veto any suggestions by the synagogue that he judged harmful to his conception.[2]

The subject he chose was ten Hebrew prophets. Although raised in a secular Jewish household, never a member of any synagogue, Landau identified with the prophets because, like him, they were concerned with justice and injustice. To him they were rebels who defended morality, independent of priests and at times even of God, whose style, the artist concluded, was anger.[3] The irony is that a "spiritual humanist," as Landau called himself—lacking a background in Jewish liturgy and observance, let alone a belief in God—created one of the great religious works of our time. As the former curator of the Philadelphia Museum of Art, Kneeland McNulty, wrote when it was completed in 1974, *The Prophetic Quest* may well mark a "significant moment" in ecclesiastical art.[4]

Viewing Landau's monumental work, we are captured not by stories but by images with an extraordinary "here-and-now presence."[5] His windows are not illustrations but visions. Nothing is merely "pleasant" or "pretty"; we are caught up in a vision that makes demands on us. Wherever we look, there is the body in action: the plunging Elijah, the writhing Job, Jeremiah boldly displaying his genitals. The artist views the human form as paradigmatic, embodying all human values, including freedom and order, hope and despair.[6]

The body asserts itself as the place where pain lives with hope. It is the nexus of human suffering and our imagination of a world free of suffering. Landau's figurative art, central to his life, had always cut against the grain of abstract expressionism, a movement in America that began in the 1940s and 1950s and quickly became mainstream. Landau's practice was, in effect, a protest. It was meant to incite change. Landau admitted no art that was merely decorative, merely beautiful. His manifesto: "Art not tied to individual growth, to humanity and life, is dangerous because it lulls or amuses without altering consciousness."[7]

His vision is anchored by words. In each window, word balloons offer guidance amid what initially feels like a chaos of color and line. Familiar biblical texts, such as Isaiah's "the wolf shall dwell with the lamb" (11:6), comfort the viewer.[8] Verbal-visual images slash the colors like thought-daggers, as when Abraham confronts God himself: "Will you indeed destroy the righteous with the wicked?" (Gen 18:23). God complains about humankind in Amos and exalts the man Job. These texts provide an anchor in a sea of color. And certainly, standing before *The Prophetic Quest* in Keneseth Israel synagogue, we can say with the biblical Jacob, "How full of awe is this place!"[9]

The Windows in the Artist's Life

Landau's designs for the windows were hard-won. They emerged from a long history of questioning himself as a man and artist in the world. From the day the principal of his Philadelphia grammar school gave him a bottle of Higgins India ink, precipitating, as the artist later said, a "crisis of self-awareness," Landau became an active explorer and questioner of himself and the world. At the age of twelve he roamed the city, capturing everything in his sketchbook, from zoo animals to street vendors. But when he was a teenager, it was the jobless men in the streets and the lonely men on the subways who moved him. They aroused the kind of anger that he saw in Amos, raging at those who "trample upon the needy" (8:4–6). Out of such experiences arose the artist's fundamental sense of injustice in the world.[10]

This set the trajectory of a lifelong struggle to achieve self-understanding as an artist: from hero combating injustice (1930s–1940s), to witness proclaiming the darkness within and without (1950s–1960s), to prophet reconciling both roles (end of the 1960s). Each of these achievements in self-understanding was an episode, often painful, in the life of an artist who believed that art could have an impact on the way people think and act, but only if the artist's life itself became a "tale of self-conquest." Identifying with Dante, who had to go through hell to gain paradise, Landau believed that to fulfill his calling as an artist he had to go through his "own apocalypse of awakening." To get beyond anguish, he had to "gain a heightened awareness of the meaning of love as a shared experience," as a "counter-force to the violence of the world." The challenge was to maintain hope and love in the face of suffering. If his crises of self-awareness were necessary to Landau's discovery of who he was as a man, his struggles to achieve the conquest of self were integral to fulfilling his responsibility as an artist.[11]

The artist's commitment to the human—our actions and bodies at risk—and to the meaning of our stories of fear, conflict, and hope remained with Landau. It was the continuous thread not only of his intellectual and emotional development but also of his artistic development. This commitment was deepened by his meeting in 1945 with survivors of Buchenwald. For the rest of his life, the Holocaust sat on Landau's shoulder like an "incubus" he could not exorcise.[12] And the body in pain seared his heart when, a couple of years later, he visited the German painter Matthias Grünewald's Isenheim altarpiece. The artist's deeply moving expression of bodily suffering was to haunt Landau throughout his career.[13]

After the Holocaust, the world was simply a darker place for the artist. Landau turned away from dreams of social progress and human perfectibility toward a profound sense of the tragic. The reality of the Holocaust put his conquest of the self, maintaining hope in the face of violence, to the test. Consequently, his last artistic phase, during which the monumental windows were completed, dealt with injustice.[14] We understand why *The Prophetic Quest* was a defining work. Landau was now explicitly identifying himself with the prophets. The entire curve of the artist's life bent toward revealing the injustice of the world and speaking out against it.

Landau's Dialog with the Prophets

In preparation for his Keneseth Israel project, Landau immersed himself in the writings of the Hebrew prophets. He learned first that prophecy was largely devoted to protesting the follies of the day. Contrary to popular belief, the prophet does not predict the future but reveals the present, calling out injustice, condemning it, and proclaiming alternative directions. Isaiah's words pierced the artist's heart: "Seek justice, undo oppression" (1:17). And hope lies in knowing that another path can be chosen.[15]

Landau spent nearly a year studying the prophets and various commentaries on them, in particular Martin Buber's *The Prophetic Faith* and Carl Jung's *Answer to Job*. Landau discovered that the prophets struggled, as he did, for self-awareness, in an effort to establish themselves not only as men but also as prophets. As a result of his intense study, Landau began to view himself not as a hero, or merely a witness, but as an artist-prophet who, like Isaiah, shapes his images into an ingenious "manifoldness" of meaning.[16] Buber's influence may have led Landau to include Job in *The Prophetic Quest* as a prophet, which was not traditional. Buber understood Job's confrontation with God as a prophetic experience, calling him a "faithful rebel" like Abraham and Isaiah.[17]

But Job challenged Landau like no other prophet, because this innocent man does not shy away from a serious charge against God himself. Job does not ask why terrible things happened to him, but rather how these actions can be squared with the God whom Job thought he knew. Buber points out that Ezekiel answers this question directly and disturbingly: whatever the secret of reward and punishment, the reality is that God destroys *both* the righteous and the wicked (Ezek 21:8 [JPS]; Job 9:22). But Job denies Ezekiel's dogmatic assertion, and this is the interpretation that Landau suggests in their respective windows. He makes Ezekiel a static, bound figure anchored in bones, while Job flows upward, blossoming into a baby who looks to the future. Countering Ezekiel, Job questions whether suffering, which God inflicts "gratuitously," can be reconciled with a just God. Studying Job, Landau came to reject God's explanation to Job that there are two kinds of justice—earthly justice exhibited in mankind's social interactions and divine justice distributed in creation. Job's religion offers a reasonable God, Buber reminded Landau, but Job does not recognize this God either in his own life or in the world.[18]

After conversing with the prophets for almost year, Landau came to realize that even God appears to lack self-awareness and struggles for self-conquest. Frighteningly unpredictable, the God of the prophets is a paradoxical, self-contradictory divinity, which is why so much anxiety underlies the books of the prophets. The prophets possessed a greater self-awareness, in fact, than God. In Jung's view, Job, for example, is "superior to his divine partner" both intellectually and morally, a view Landau came to agree with.[19] Again, he points to Amos, "Shall there be evil in the city and the Lord hath not done it?" (3:6).[20] Yet Jung does not perceive God as evil. He is the totality of justice *and* injustice. Listening closely to the prophets, Landau concluded that these were not opposites but what Blake called "contraries," equally true and mutually essential, vital to making any progress in self-understanding.[21]

Out of Dialog, Landau's Vision

The radical new form of these windows—their commitment to the body and its incarnation in slashing fragments of colored glass—emerges, Landau confessed, from a deep layer of "feeling and dream."[22] The layers derived from his dialog with the prophets, out of which he created his vision of the quest for justice and "dreams for a just order."[23] This was paramount in his mind from the outset. In his formal prospectus for the windows presented to Keneseth Israel, he stated that his central theme may be titled "The Prophetic Quest."[24] The story told in the windows is simply the quest for justice, from Abraham to Malachi. This the artist makes his own and desires to make ours.

But why this particular group of prophets in this order—Abraham, Elijah, Amos, Hosea, Isaiah, Jeremiah, Ezekiel, Second Isaiah, Job, and Malachi? Abraham and Job are not traditionally regarded as prophets. Neither is included in the division of the Hebrew Bible devoted to the prophets: Abraham appears in the Torah (the Five Books of Moses, or Pentateuch) and Job in the Writings (poetic books). A good case is often made for Abraham as a prophet but not for Job. Landau insists on them both, however, and pivots on these "prophets," rather than on a major one like Isaiah. For it is Abraham who asks God if he is just, and it is Job's God who replies. Their positioning in his sequence, which is chronological, questions not only man's justice but God's.[25] And though Isaiah, Jeremiah, and Ezekiel are central to the succession, the windows accord them no special status. The five major prophets that Landau chooses (Elijah, Isaiah, Jeremiah, Ezekiel, Second Isaiah) and three minor ones (Hosea, Amos, Malachi), all speaking for a God challenged by Abraham and Job, are on an equal plane.

Abraham–Elijah introduces *The Prophetic Quest*, echoed by the Job–Malachi pair at the end. The Hebrew words that Landau selects for the first window haunt each of the succeeding prophets: "Shall not the Judge of all the earth do justly?" (Gen 18:25). The Job window answers the Abraham window: *No*, God does not always act justly, and thus the hand of the Abraham window can be seen as the hand of the Accuser, who is Satan in the book of Job. And the Malachi window answers the Elijah window: *Yes*, man can turn from injustice and embrace justice. This *yes* is fraught, however, because there can be no guarantee from God. We are given a promise in Malachi, but it remains for humans to fulfill the promise. In the end the question of justice raised by the first pair of prophets is not so much answered as intensified by the last.

Landau's carefully chosen title warns us against reducing his vision to one message, a single interpretation of the prophets. The artist was adamant that the windows are not merely a series of illustrations of biblical texts. By the same token, they are not expressions of orthodoxies but visionary extensions of the artist.[26] Pointedly, to emphasize struggle and movement, he called his work "The Prophetic *Quest*," not "The Prophetic *Word*" or "The Prophetic *Message*," titles suggested by members of the synagogue.[27] Reading the Jeremiah window, for example, one rabbi interprets Jeremiah's half-hidden face at the bottom of the second panel (from the top) as obscured by flames pouring from his mouth. Yet the fixed eyes and mask-like head suggest the reverse—the flames of destruction pouring onto Jeremiah if Judah shuns justice. Clearly, Landau's images suggest a reading of the prophet that cuts across the normative tradition of biblical interpretation.[28]

We are less tempted to search for a single, "true" meaning if we view *The Prophetic Quest* as midrash. An ancient Jewish approach to interpretation, midrash responds to scripture with parables and even imagined exchanges between biblical characters such as Isaiah and Ezekiel. It revels in the manifold meanings of sacred texts like Isaiah's ingenious writings. Midrash does not attempt to *clarify* scripture so much as to *create* meaning, a mission it shares with the artist. It is this meaning, delivering the force of the prophetic word, that leads to action in the world.[29] And we remember that Landau's artistic mission was not to amuse but to alter consciousness. In the alternative reading of the window above, which sees the possibility that Jeremiah could be defeated by injustice, we feel how vulnerable the prophet is to the overwhelming flames of injustice. And in opening up the prophetic writings, the artist hopes that they may brace us on our own quest for justice, strengthening us for action.

Out of Dialog, Landau's Art

Dialoging with the prophets, Landau discovered the profound nature of their quest for justice, but he also took a cue from Ezekiel's strange behavior about how to communicate this. Ezekiel picks up a stick and writes on it. He picks up another and writes on it. Strange. Then he joins them into one stick and holds it up for the people, an emblem of the tribes of Joseph and of Judah restored to one nation (37:16–22), its image-word power evident. Ezekiel's composite method, bestowed on him by God himself, was not lost on Landau. And given his youthful experience as a comic-book artist, drawing Captain America, this is not surprising. Such experience informs *The Prophetic Quest* throughout. We see everywhere a fictitious space free of gravity, typical of comic-book art, in which the prophets appear. But it is word balloons, which virtually define the comic book, that complete the parallel. And Landau carefully orchestrates their positioning from window to window, demanding that we attend to the text, the words of the prophet.[30]

The prophets themselves, their postures and gestures suggesting comic-book heroes, dominate the visual space, from the cosmic giant Elijah visiting our world to the all-powerful Jeremiah striding into our city. The windows' waves of images are energized by the prophets' bodies. The artist-prophet knows that here hope resides. The hero's body is our own, imagined as free and powerful. And we know that what can be imagined can be realized. We know that the human body is the locus of both suffering and imagination, of the consequences of injustice and the vision of a world free of injustice. Isaiah knew this intimately, going naked and barefoot as a sign of the imminent punishment of Egypt (20:2–3).

Painfully aware that the body is ultimately at stake in the struggle for justice, Landau's interpretation of the biblical prophets demanded a visionary art. Seeing the artist's exquisitely modulated distortions, such as the disturbing head of Jeremiah, and dissonances of color such as the clash of oranges, greens, reds, blues, and purples in Second Isaiah, we feel Landau's pain. At the same time, we feel the intellectual edge and emotional power of his forms and images, and we sense Landau's sheer joy in forming in stained glass a visionary response to injustice.[31] Controlling the energy of his windows' color vibrations in a constantly changing light, unlike any other medium, their rhythm enhanced and amplified by the sensuous blacklines of leading that play off his colors: this is the artist's great triumph.[32]

Landau's windows were not intended to promote the sanctuary as a place primarily of introspection or contemplation, in the manner of Abraham Rattner's abstract Loop Synagogue windows in Chicago (1960), titled *The Journey of a Mystic*. Nor were Landau's windows intended to serve a mere supporting role in the synagogue's function as a house of assembly, prayer, and study. Rather, the artist of *The Prophetic Quest* wanted the introspection born in the sanctuary to be translated into action by the power of his windows. Assembled individuals, identifying with the prophets, were to go forth with a renewed commitment to justice.[33]

In this desire to inspire activism, Landau felt a kinship with Ben Shahn, whose ideals of social justice and regard for the Hebrew prophets he shared. Five years earlier, Shahn had designed two stained glass expressionist windows based on Job for Temple Beth Zion in Buffalo, New York (1965–66). Like Landau, Shahn includes a quote from the prophet in one of his windows. Significantly, however, Shahn chooses God's answer out of the whirlwind (Job 38:1–4), while Landau shifts the focus from God's exhortation to Job's ambivalent response, a shift reinforced by his figurative art in contrast to Shahn's expressionist work. The scale and drama of stained glass lends itself to addressing the fundamental questions of consciousness and value with which the Jewish community has always wrestled. Clearly, both artists continue this tradition.[34]

Landau's contribution to the evolution of modern synagogue art was the stained glass windows. He was acutely aware, as was Shahn, that art could help assure the survival of Jewish identity and faith.[35] And like him, Landau sometimes juxtaposes disparate images, traditional and contemporary, such as rock bands and prophets. But his art, as noted earlier, was informed not so much by the God concept as by the *prophet-human* concept. Landau undoubtedly knew the various treatments of the Hebrew prophets by other modern artists, but counter to prevailing trends in synagogue art, his objective was not primarily to "awaken an intrinsically religious feeling" or to "literally create the idea of the Holy."[36]

Landau rejected what his friend Leonard Baskin called "art that does not bleed when we prick it."[37] To achieve art that bleeds, piercing us with the recognition of man's fragility and suffering, both Landau and Baskin eschewed abstract expressionist Jewish synagogue art. They explicitly condemned its devaluing of figural humanism.[38]

Landau, by rejecting expressionism, asserts a humanism of action, one that is less concerned about evoking the past than provoking the future. His defiantly figurative prophets and their words not only portray fundamental individual, bodily, and social tensions, but in the prophets' quest for justice he extends the range of these tensions and probes more complex emotional and ethical dimensions.

At first we may experience the dissonances of Landau's visionary art as stressful, an emotion we would not normally expect in a sanctuary of peace and prayer, but he believed such a reaction only "heightens awareness."[39] Finding ourselves in the presence of the truly new in this world, Landau asks that we make companions of these images, to claim them as our own.[40] As it was for the prophets, so it was for him. It is not enough to simply record injustice; we are required to act. Imagine an alternative world, the prophets exhort us, and then work toward realizing it—"Seek justice, relieve the oppressed" (Isa 1:17 [JPS]).

The Windows

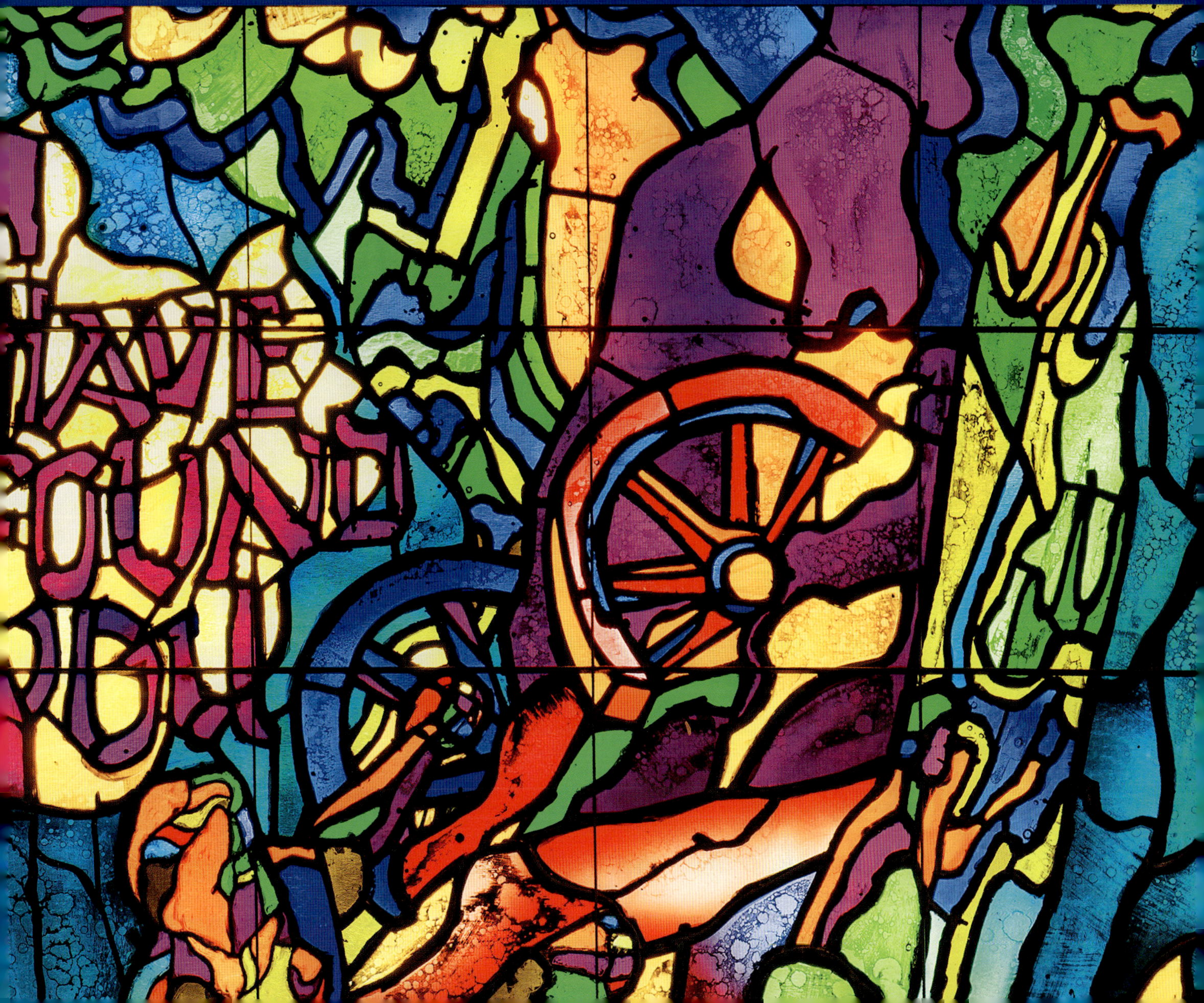

Interpretive Commentary

David S. Herrstrom

Just as a musical note depends on the phrase in which it lives, the meaning of an image depends on its context—so too the grand symphony of *The Prophetic Quest*. Colors, forms, and images carried by Landau's melodic lines create a rhythmic pattern that he calls its wave-form, pulsing from window to window. Throughout, as our perspective continually shifts with these waves, our understanding of justice deepens.[1]

Two sets of prophets frame the *Quest*. It starts with Abraham–Elijah and ends with Job–Malachi. Both Abraham and Job challenge God's morality. Abraham asks God, "Will You indeed destroy the righteous with the wicked?" (Gen 18:23). And he bargains with God, who in turn, in the end, submits to bargaining with Job. Complementing this unresolved question is the promise of a future redemption, pointed to by both Elijah and Malachi. But by pairing Job and Malachi at the end, Landau challenges the traditional belief that earthly justice flows from the eternal God.

The *Quest* comprises two main waves. Flanking the sanctuary are five windows on a side—on our left, facing the ark at the front, Abraham to Isaiah; on the right, Jeremiah to Malachi. Landau insisted that the windows move from back to front *on both sides*, emphasizing that they constitute separate waves. To reinforce this, the background colors of opposite windows correspond—the red of Abraham echoing the red of Jeremiah, likewise the green, orange, and blue of Isaiah resonating with that of Malachi. More important, Landau defines the wave on the left by transforming the tree of knowledge in Abraham's window to the tree of life in Isaiah's. And in the wave on the right, Jeremiah's mask becomes Malachi's portrait, their penetrating eyes undimmed. The first wave questions whether justice lies in God's hands; the second, whether it lies in ours.[2]

Each image that we experience in a given moment of looking is an unexpected confrontation. And this represents the prophetic insight. As Landau insisted, this unsettling experience is essential to the struggle for justice. Yet we are continually aware, as Rabbi Korn has said, that these windows also grace the synagogue with the "holiness of beauty. They have bestowed indescribable glories of color and form and movement and light upon us and upon all those who through the years will enter here to meditate, to weep, to rejoice, or simply to drink in the glowing radiance and warmth of this splendid artistry."[3]

The panels of the windows are numbered top to bottom: 1–6. Panel numbers are given first in the word, figure, and object listings that precede each of the commentaries. When they are mentioned in the commentary itself, the panel numbers and biblical citations follow. For biblical quotations, Landau used both the Jewish Publication Society (JPS) and the King James (KJV) translations (sometimes a combination of the two); chapter and verse citations are separated by a colon.

First wave of windows: Abraham to Isaiah (left to right). Photo © 2013 Tom Crane Photography.

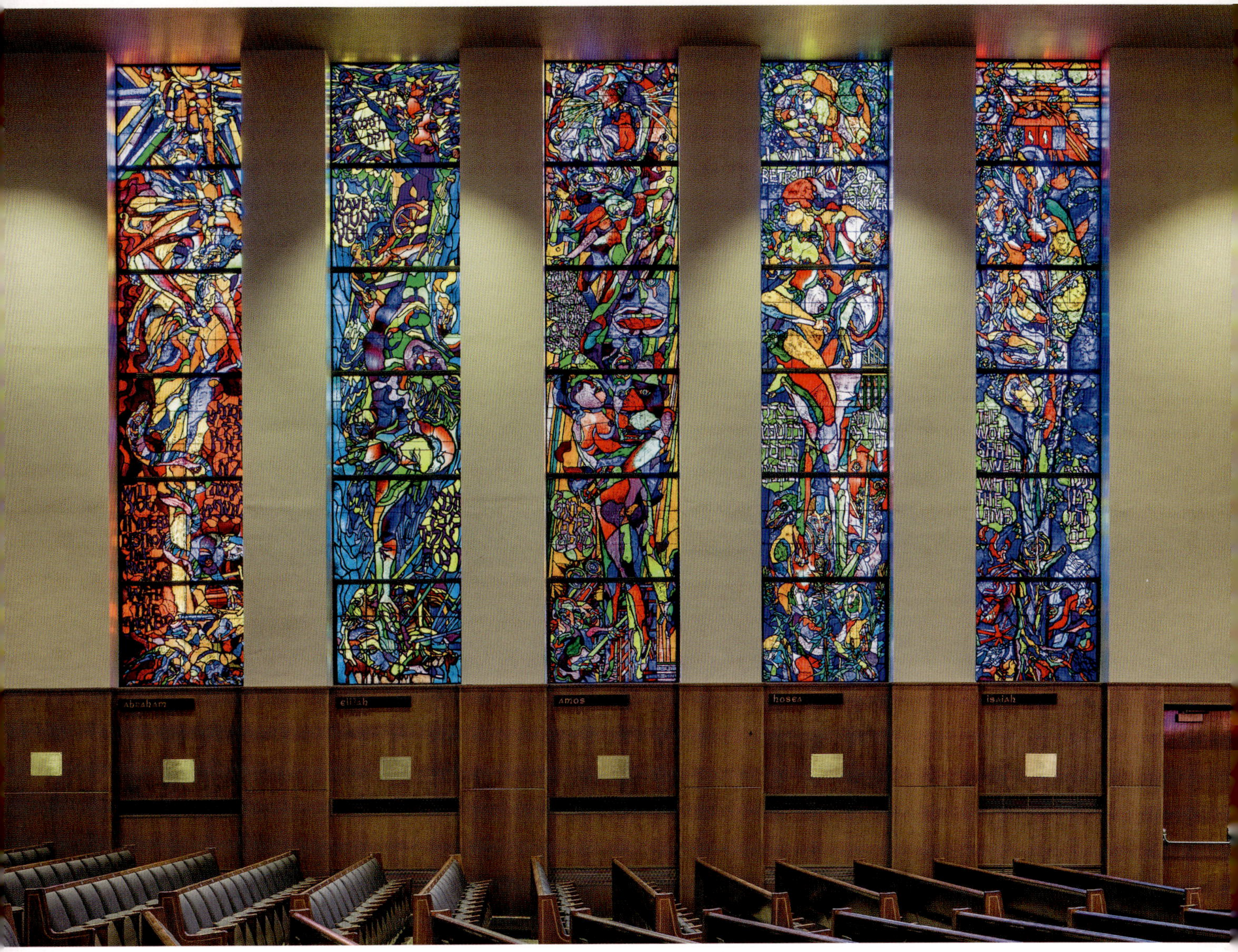
abraham
elijah
amos
hosea
isaiah

Abraham

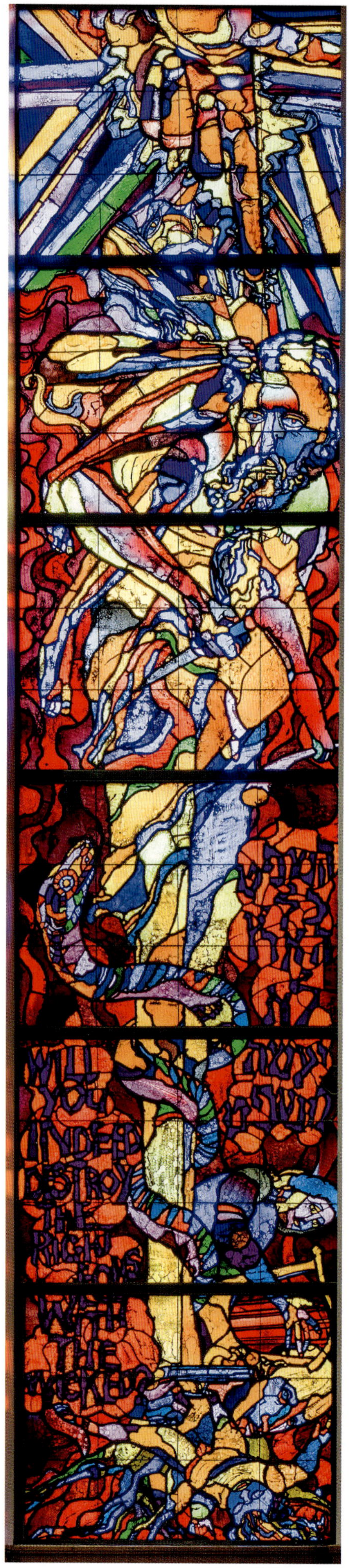

WORDS: (4–5, Heb) Shall not the Judge of all the earth do justly? (Gen 18:25); (5–6, Eng) Will you indeed destroy the righteous with the wicked? (Gen 18:23)

FIGURES: (1) hand pointing downward; (2–3) Abraham with his elderly wife Sarah on his back, face concealed, her fist pressed against Abraham's head and her legs angled over his shoulder; (2–3) Abraham's arm reaching from between her legs and holding a knife at Isaac's back; (3–4) Isaac emerging from Abraham's loins, looking upward and holding a ram's horn; (5–6) David playing his harp; (6) the faces of two figures, the one above crying out in pain, the one below with his head back and eyes closed in death

OBJECTS: (1–6) the trunk of the tree, which becomes (4–6) Abraham's body encircled by a serpent; (5–6, Eng) word balloon on the left and (4–5, Heb) on the right; (6) hand pointing a pistol to the right

When Abraham learns that God is about to destroy the city of Sodom, he is appalled and asks, "Will You indeed destroy the righteous with the wicked?" (Gen 18:23). By substituting the word "indeed" for the King James' "also," Landau calls attention to his shock. His words capture *The Prophetic Quest's* central question of justice and its origin. The artist dramatizes Abraham's challenge visually by emphasizing God's reaction to it—his accusing finger aimed directly at the prophet's head. Echoing this image, a pistol threatens a man at the bottom of the window.

Abraham's sad, perplexed countenance becomes ours as in our mind God's hand becomes a threatening pistol. David has turned on his side to play his harp as if to lament the fate of the rising Isaac, about to be sacrificed to God's "justice." And Abraham's dagger of death exactly parallels the ram's horn of life that Isaac holds. Which will prevail?

The answer is uncertain, because we are left with God's reply to Abraham in a word balloon (Heb) accompanied by the deceitful serpent in Eden: "Shall not the Judge of all the earth do justly?" An open question at this point, as the snake entwining the tree of knowledge in a red field of blood—being shed or giving life—means the possibility to choose evil, exile, and death over life (Gen 2:9).

The central conflict of the Abraham window is reinforced by tension between Isaac's upward thrust against the hand's downward accusation, which is reversed in the next window, Elijah, with the prophet's plunge countered by his chariot's rise. These counter-movements are echoed by Job and Malachi at the end of the *Quest*.

Traditionally, earthly justice was assumed to flow from the eternal God, but by insisting on Job as a prophet and pairing him with Malachi, Landau offers another vision. For Job echoes Abraham's challenge to God while Malachi echoes Elijah's call for redemption, the "still, small voice" of God (1 Kings 19:12) that Landau calls simply our human voice of "conscience."

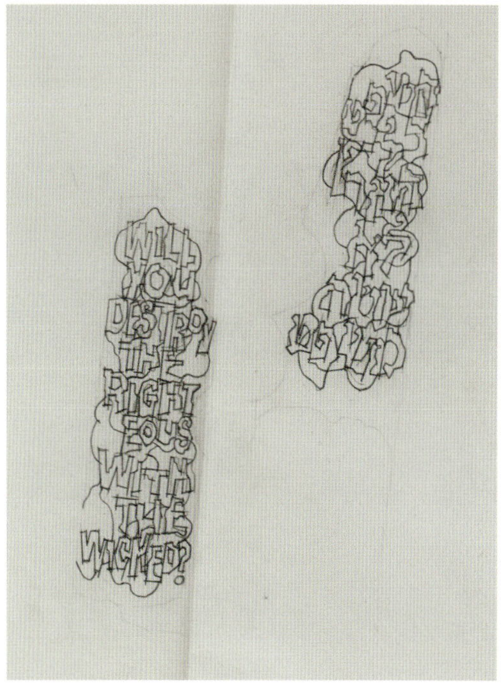

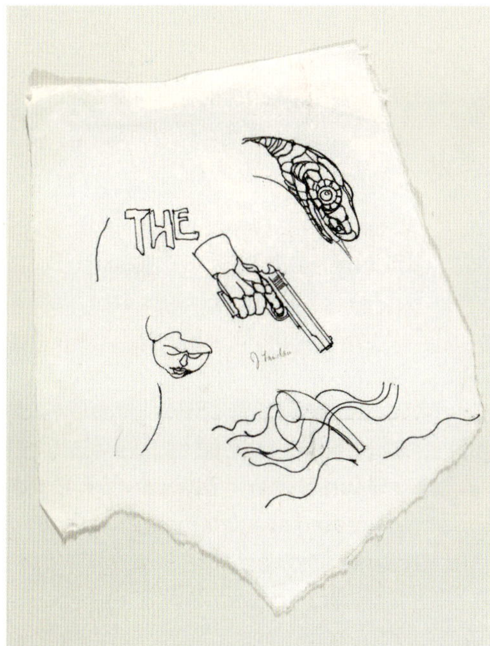

TOP In his final word balloon (panel 5) Landau adds the word "INDEED," emphasizing the gravity of Abraham's question addressed to God. Jacob Landau Collection, Monmouth University Galleries. Courtesy of Monmouth University.

BOTTOM Originally Landau put a pistol in Abraham's hand (panel 3), which symbolized the "sacrificing of young men" in Vietnam. But at the Art Committee's request, he replaced it with the dagger and, not willing to give up the pistol, moved it to the bottom (panel 6). Woodmere Art Museum: Gift of Rosa T. Giletti, 2015. Courtesy of the Woodmere Art Museum.

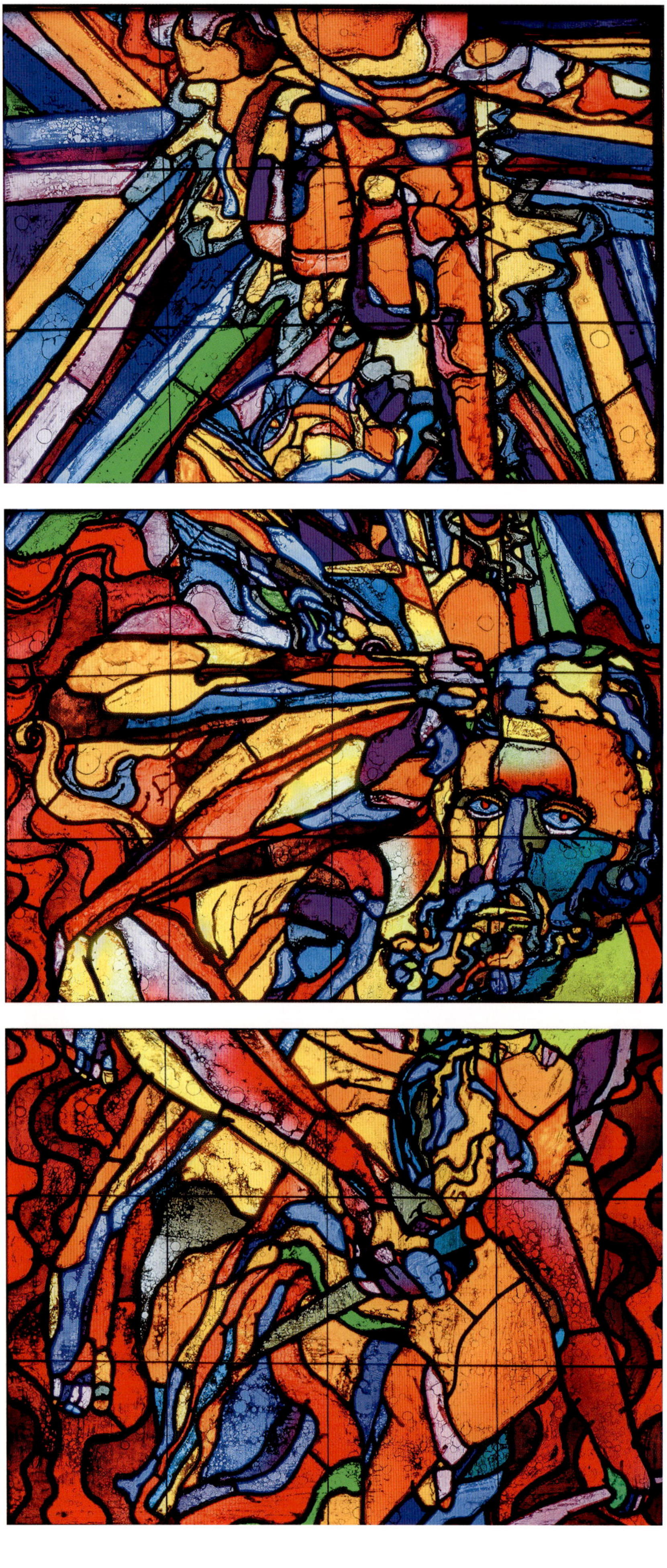

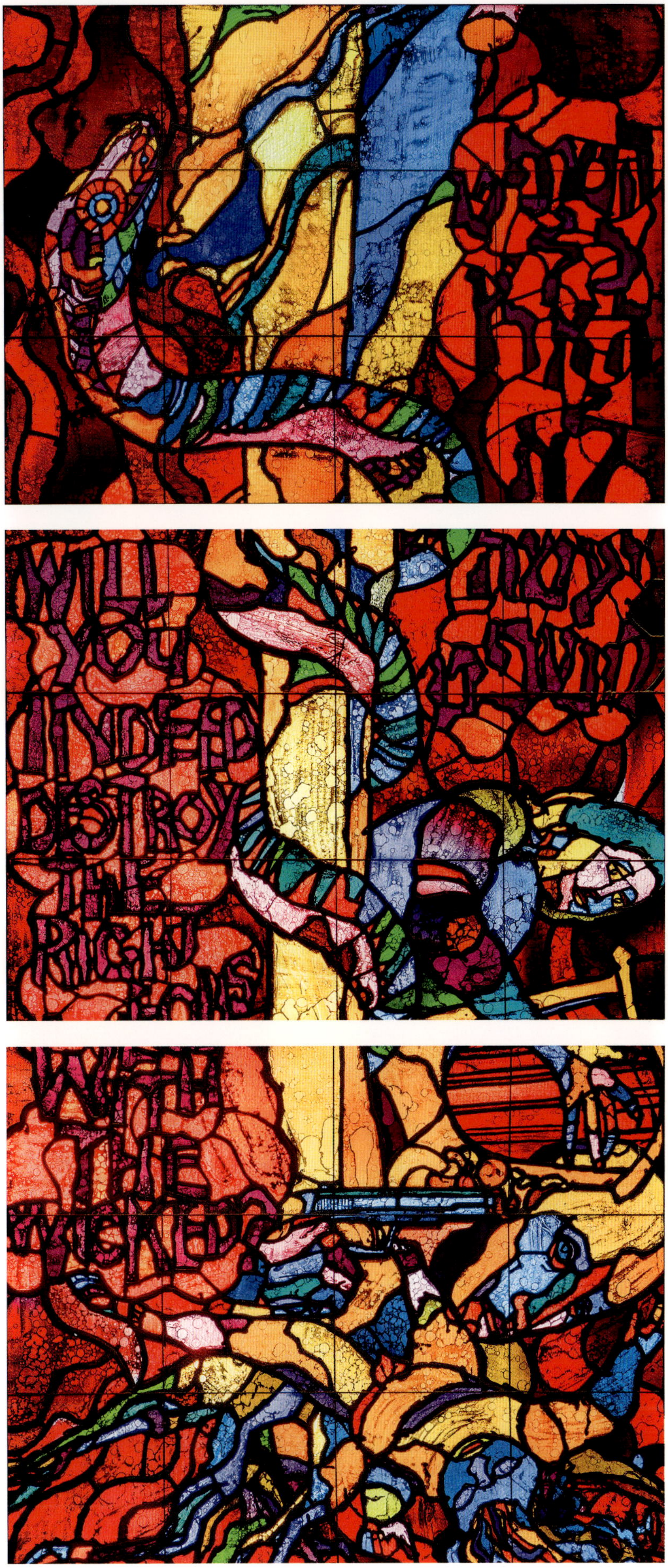
WILL
YOU
INDEED
DESTROY
THE
WITH
THE
WICKED

Elijah

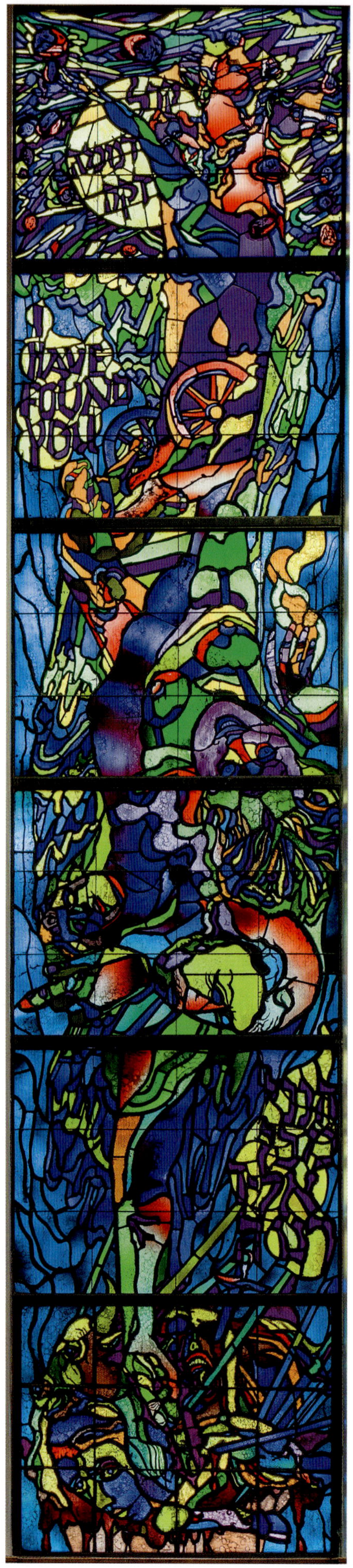

1
2
3
4
5
6

WORDS: (1, Heb) The still, small voice (1 Kings 19:12); (2, Eng) I have found you (1 Kings 21:20); (5, Heb) Behold, I will bring evil upon you (1 Kings 21:21)

FIGURES*:* (1–2) Elijah in his chariot with his arm raised across a word balloon, (1–3) his right arm and mantle billowing upward with the whirlwind into heaven,[4] and (5–6) his left arm and hand reaching downward and grasping the earth; (3) Jezebel inverted with her hand stretching upward and (4) her hair hanging down; (4) Ahab's harlequin head beside Elijah; (6) living head on a sacrificial altar (6)

OBJECTS: (1, Heb) sun as word balloon; (1–4) Elijah's mantle; (2) chariot wheels rolling over Jezebel's body; (2, Eng) word balloon on the left and (5, Heb) on the right; (6) sacrificial bull

Abraham's question—Will God deal justly with man?—becomes, in this window, Will man deal justly with man? This question is explored more fully in the five windows opposite. Here the world of human justice is turned upside down. Elijah facing downward is pitted against Jezebel facing upward (3). Their heads dominate the middle of the window, their equal size dramatizing the conflict between Jezebel's choosing evil, her injustice in having Naboth killed so Ahab can possess his vineyard, and Elijah's choosing justice, punishing Jezebel and holding the soil of life as the rains come (6).

These two contrary forces energize the window, its action bursting from the center. Jezebel's face is an unfeeling mask, turned away from Elijah's compassionate face. And her body breaks up, while his with its trailing mantle ties earth to heaven. If God's justice is challenged in the Abraham window, Man's is challenged in this window; together they raise the question that launches the quest's waves: Can there be justice in heaven or earth?

That Elijah's chariot destroys Jezebel raises the hope that the answer is affirmative. After all, Elijah ascends through violence into the golden circle, where from the sun (a perfect word balloon) we hear the "still, small voice" of God. In our world, however, Elijah speaks out loudly against injustice, telling Ahab, who has sold himself "to work evil" (1 Kings 21:20), "I have found you." And this word balloon (2) exactly balances that carrying the words of justice, "I will bring evil upon you" (5).

Yet the sun may be setting or about to be overcome by storms. The world above is not only silent but verging on disorder, which the artist's slashes and fragments of color imply. Disorder likewise threatens the world below, with its dissonant colors that even Landau's black lattice (6) cannot control.

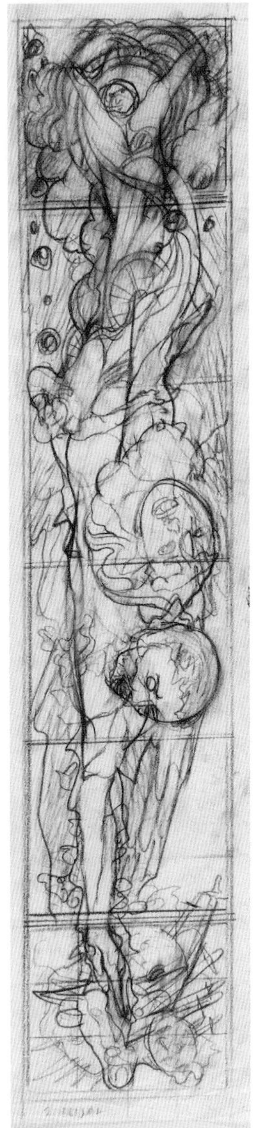

TOP Drawing for Elijah. Woodmere Art Museum: Gift of Rosa T. Giletti, 2015. Courtesy of the Woodmere Art Museum.

BOTTOM Draft of English and Hebrew lettering. From the private collection of Rosa T. Giletti.

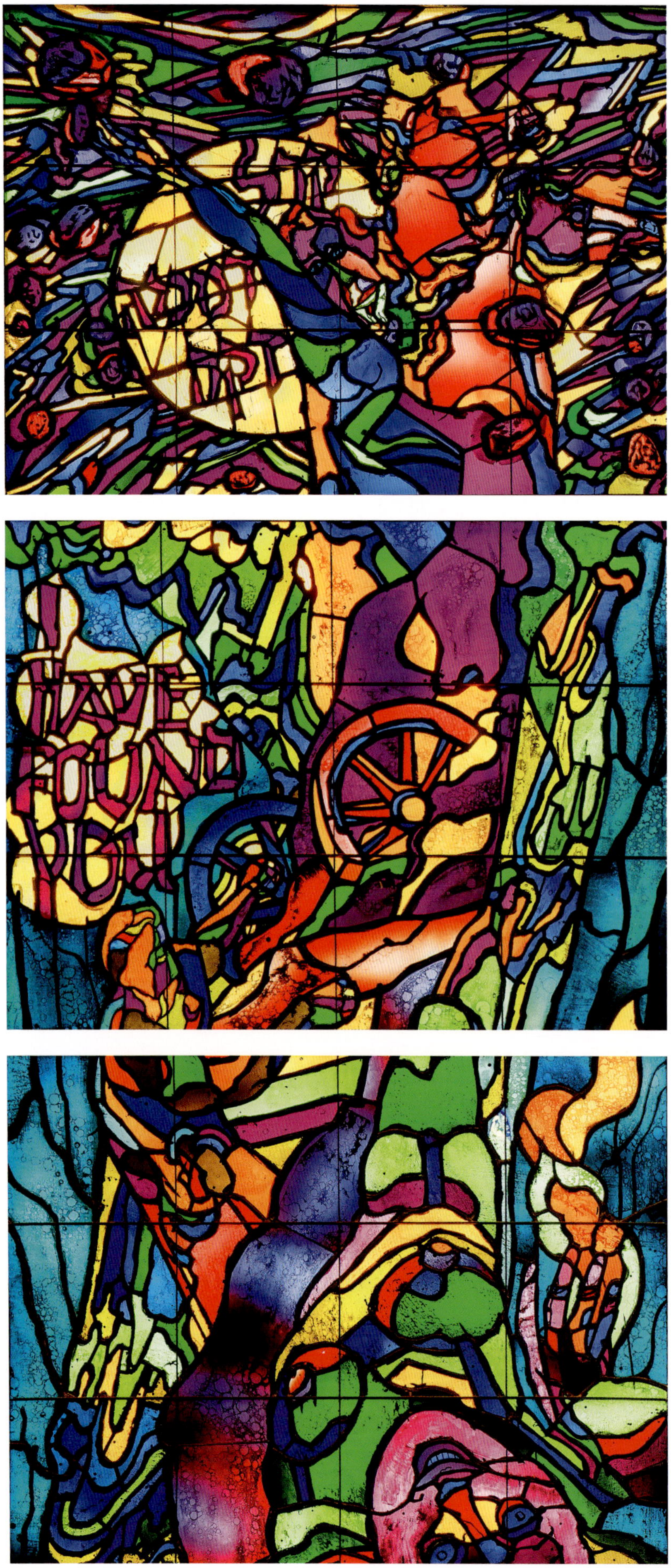

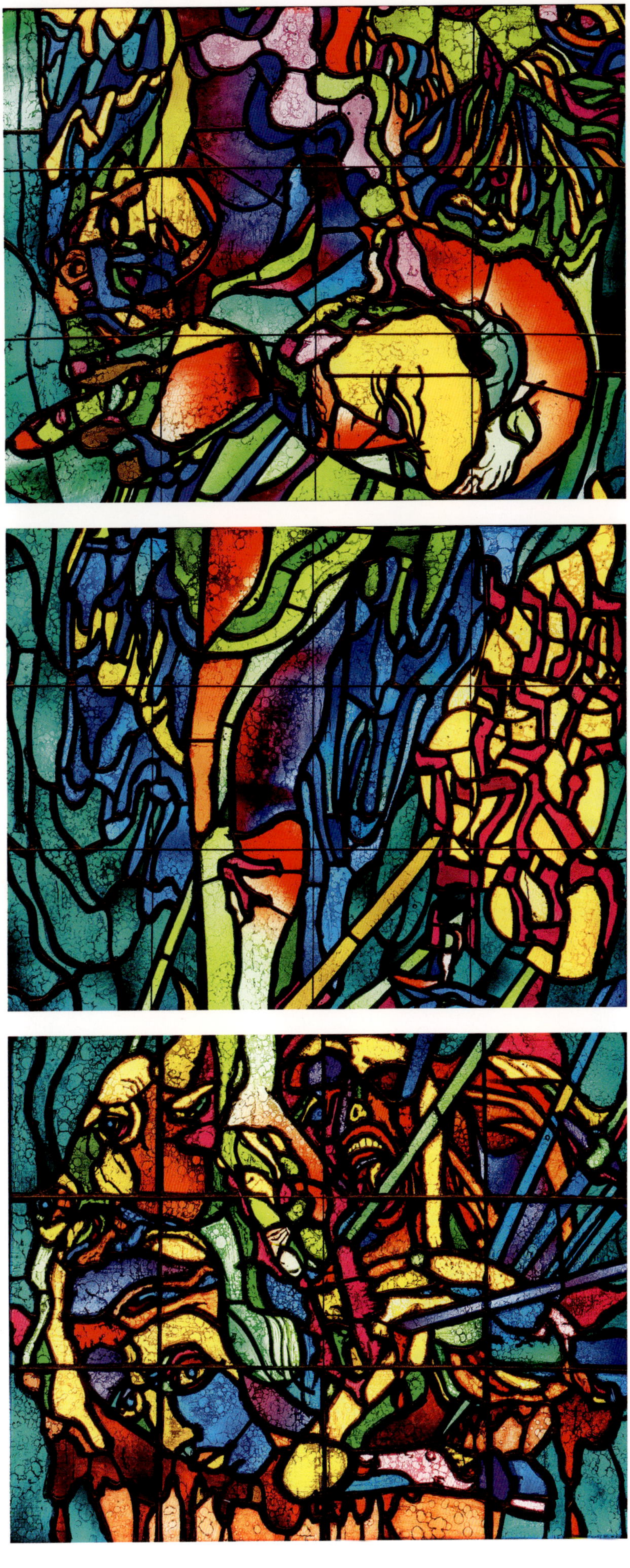

Amos

WORDS: (3, Eng) Take away from me the noise of your songs (5:23); (5, Heb) Let justice well up as waters, and righteousness as a mighty stream (5:24)

FIGURES: (1–2) angry Amos as a beast-man with a prophet's steely eyes to the left of a lion; (2) man in an athlete's pose turned away from the beast-man and reaching down with his right arm to touch the word balloon (Eng), his head and left arm bent, and knee raised; (2) head of a man to our left looking over the athlete's head and raising his right hand, either in fright or in anger at the beast-man above him; (3) TV-man with blood-red tongue; (3–4) man in sunglasses with an open mouth displaying multicolored teeth, (2–3) his exaggerated right arm raised to the downward-reaching arm of the athlete above; (4) prostitute displaying her pink breasts, held in the arms of a bear-man whose (5) hand, behind which lurks a sinister face, gestures toward the word balloon (Heb), (5–6) their legs extending into the musicians' scene; (6) guitarist and singer

OBJECTS: (1–6) fire glowing orange in the background; (1) giant head of a roaring lion with an outsized mouth and tongue (1–2) surrounded by small disembodied eyes; (5–6) two raised trombones; (6) guitar; (6) section of a light-show support grid; (6) two factory smokestacks

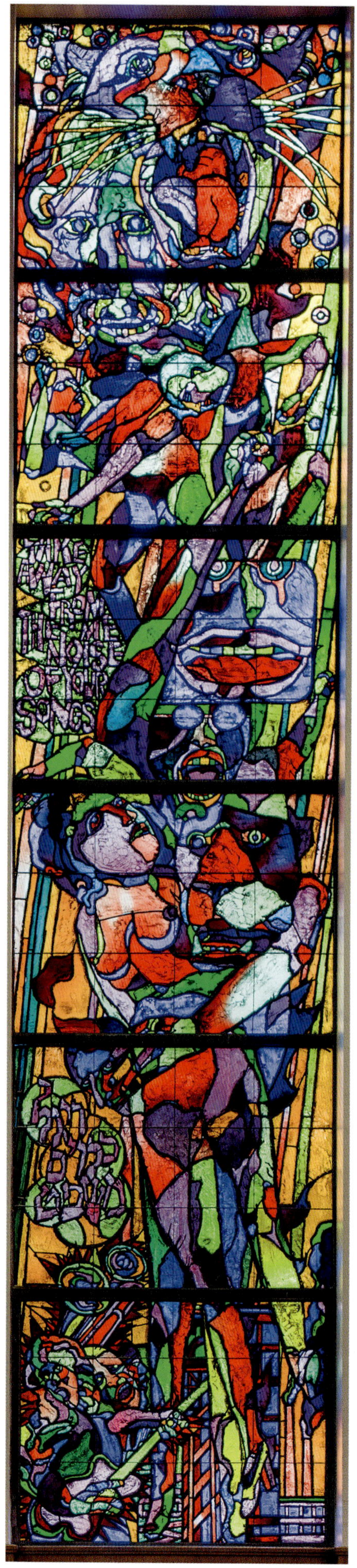

1

2

3

4

5

6

In Landau's noisiest window—lion roaring, TV-man blaring, man in sunglasses singing, rock band performing—the words of Amos, called to our attention (2–3) by the athlete who may run away but cannot escape them (2:15), demand that the noise cease: "Take away from me the noise of your songs" (5:23). And bear-man in a compromised position with a temple prostitute[5] (4) points to the prophet's other demand, visually echoing the athlete, that "justice well up" (5:24) in the land (Heb, 4–5).

Both demands are ironic here, because in the context of the window not only is it hypocrites who point to the prophet's demands, but there is in fact no quiet and no justice. An atmosphere of disequilibrium is suggested by the artist's diagonals placed against verticals that are off plumb, skewing God's metaphoric measure of justice (7:8). Landau places Amos's challenge before us and juxtaposes it with our modern world of ads and entertainment.

We want to take seriously the lion at the top who roars out of Zion (1:2), the Lord himself accompanied by the stars of Orion (5:8). After all, the voice of Amos is his. But this fierce lion in the window's world of mockery may be a comic-book beast, surrounded not by stars but by eyes, intent on seeking out evil, strangely floating (9:8). Yet the prophet's mockery of the world given to us by the artist has at the same time a serious message: Amos finds no justice in either the religious or the secular world.

Amos mocks in earnest religion's pious songs as noise. He rages against religious hypocrites who "trample upon the needy" (8:4–6) but cannot forget that the evil in their city is the work of God (3:6). The rock band (6), which was not in the artist's original study for the window (fig. 32), underlines in fun this antiliturgical stance.[6] But this secular world is not ultimately the source of justice either. As the prophet says, we may escape the lion's mouth (God) only to meet a bear (man) (5:19). Tellingly, the secular obsessions with sex (bear-man) and entertainment (TV-man) dominate the center of the window.

In short, Amos has little patience for the questions posed by Abraham–Elijah, with their implicit hope of answers. He despairs of finding justice in either the heavenly or the earthly realm and describes terrifying visions of what continued injustice will bring.

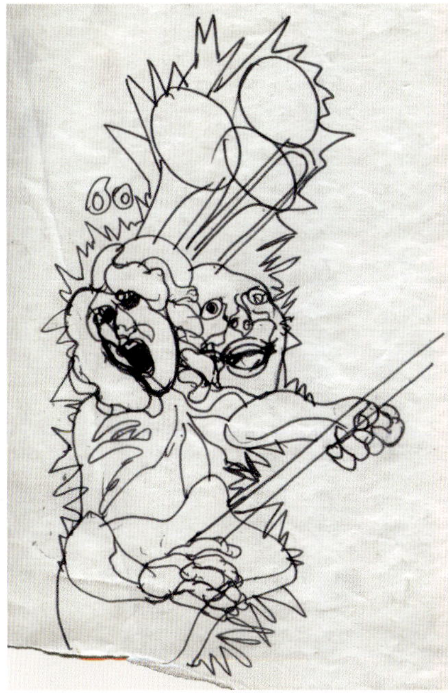

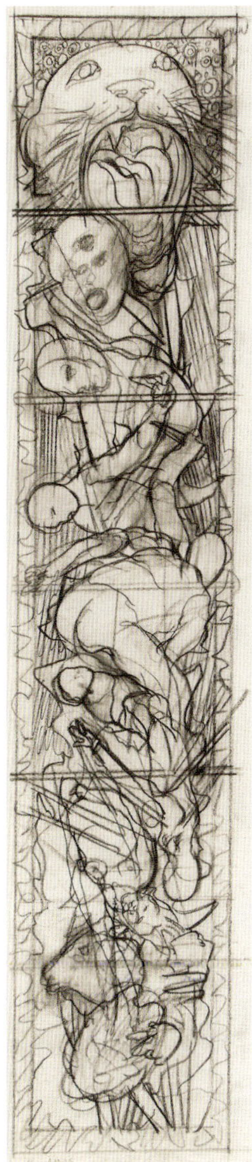

A

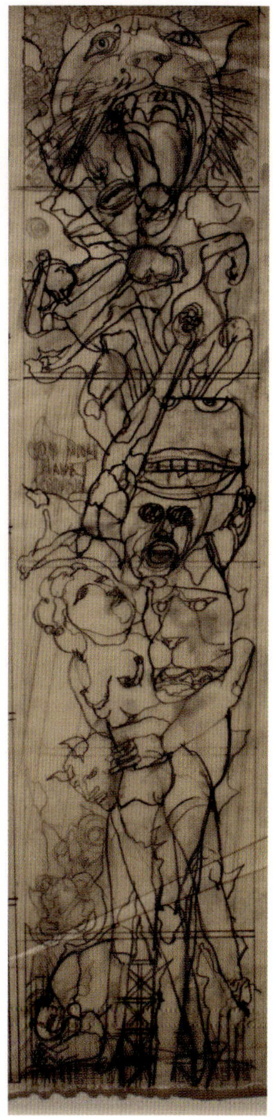

B

TOP Preliminary drawing for the band in the Amos window. Subsequent to this sketch Landau added a trombone and a singer to increase the noise. His window became even noisier when he emphasized the two trombones of his drawing and added a third singer (panel 6). Photo © 2013 Tom Crane Photography.

BOTTOM At the bottom of an early sexually explicit sketch (A), Landau did not include the rock band (later glass panel 6) or words. In a subsequent sketch (B), Landau added the band and an English text (panel 3), which did not refer to "noise" but raised doubts that justice could be found in either the religious or secular worlds: "You only have I known [... therefore I will punish you for all your iniquities]" (3:2). In a later formal drawing for this window Landau changed the text to accord with the band's "noise" (panel 3).

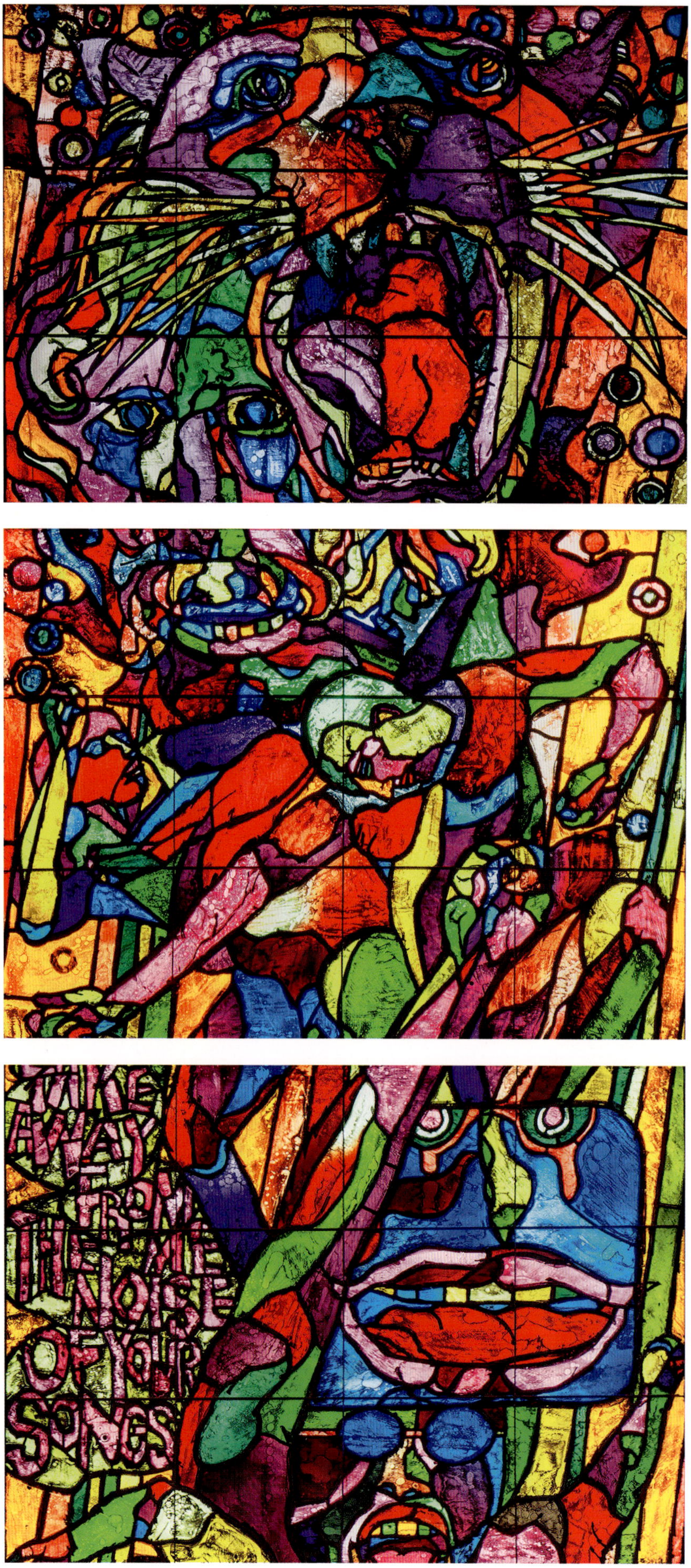
TAKE AWAY FROM ME THE NOISE OF YOUR SONGS

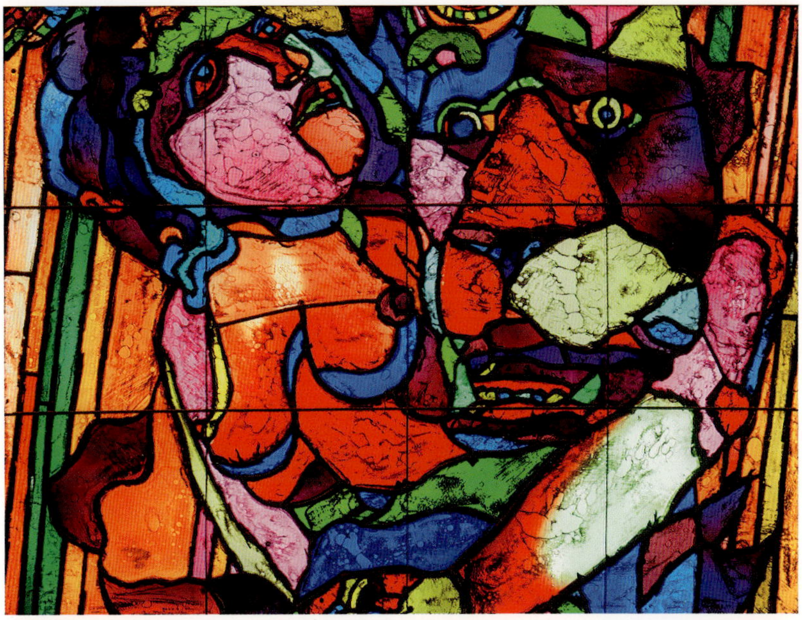

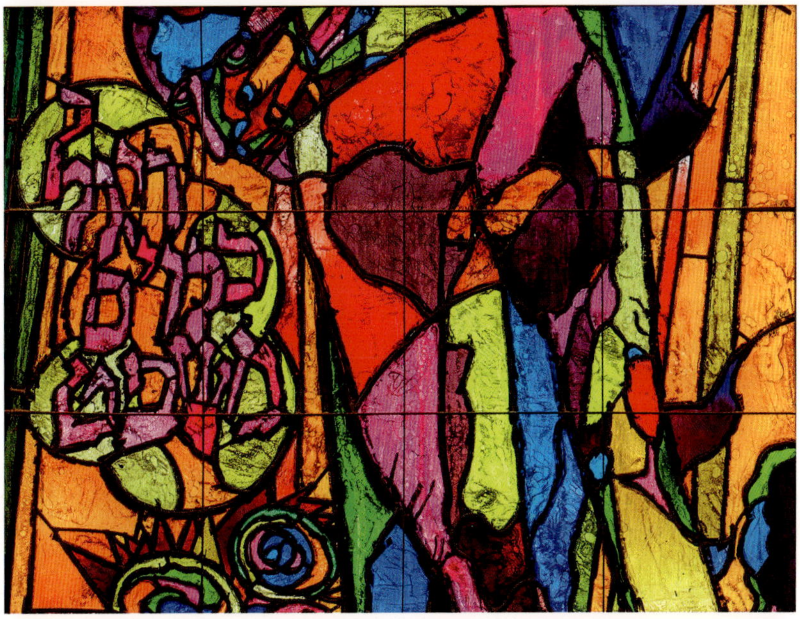

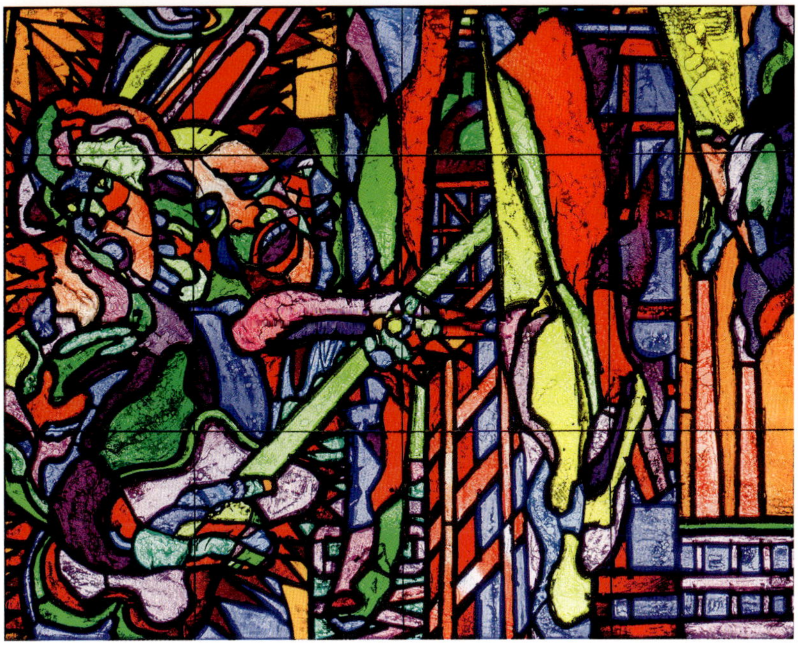

Hosea

WORDS*:* (1–2, Eng) I will betroth you to Me forever (KJV 2:19; JPS 2:21); (4, Heb) I will betroth you unto me in righteousness and justice, in loving-kindness and in compassion (2:19; 2:21)

FIGURES*:* (1) large hand bound in scriptures (phylacteries) holding a child; (2) to the left, Hosea's head in profile, bent to Gomer's head, which is turned away from him, and to the right one of their children, facing us; (3) Gomer's breast half-framed by her bent elbow, her thigh below, and to the right another of her children framed by the lozenge shape of a robe; (2–5) Hosea's torso and legs extending downward; (6) man in profile looking upward holding a pole; (5–6) to his left a man in profile with his head turned downward, and on the right a man facing us, holding a sword in his raised arm

OBJECTS*:* (1) vineyards surrounding the hand holding a child; (1–2, Eng) word balloons; (3–4) wall grating; (4, Heb) word balloons; (4–5) bull's head; (5–6) pole held upright ending in a mask; (4–5) raised sword touching the bull's head; (5) hawk's head; (6) thorns

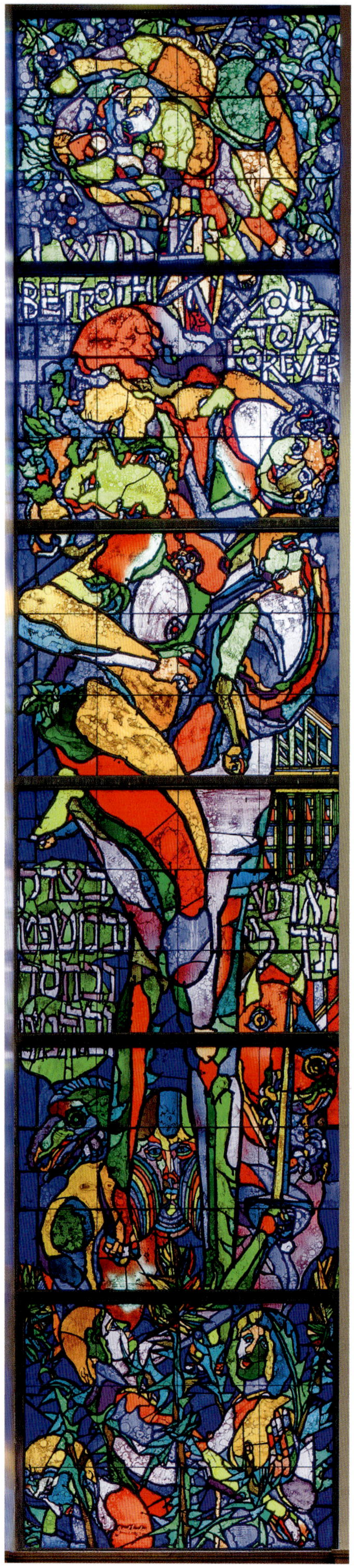

1
2
3
4
5
6

In a radical act, Hosea marries a whore named Gomer. After bearing three children, she commits adultery and he puts her away, only to take her back out of an enduring love. This is a personally tragic but also transcendent experience, for the prophet realizes that his action mirrors God's relationship with Israel, his body itself an emblem of what God has revealed about the divine character. Just as Hosea extends his loving-kindness to Gomer, so God does the same to Israel, being married to its people, who have turned from him, and longing, out of a steadfast love, to take them back.

And from this steadfast love will flow justice. The artist shows Hosea embracing Gomer even as she turns away from him, just as the people turned away from God. Priests and kings betrayed their office (5:1), countenancing all manner of pagan gods and temple prostitution, and as a result there was no justice in the House of Israel, "they break all bounds, and blood toucheth blood" (4:2). Israel can sacrifice bulls (4–5) and "ask counsel" of pagan gods (4:12)—the mask on a pole (5)—but this will not bring justice. Nor will their worship rituals bring them close to God (8:13). For justice flows only from compassion.

Emblematic of this, the tenderness expressed by the gentle curve of Hosea's head (2) is echoed in that of God's hand (1), and it makes clear that Hosea will not reject Gomer, just as God will not reject Israel. Landau emphasizes this parallel by isolating God's words "I will" in the top panel, repeating this declaration below in Hebrew. He will not let Israel destroy itself, its people suffering violence and its vineyards turning to thorns (6), for he will control his fierce anger (11:9). And out of compassion he will restore righteousness and justice, lifting up the infant close to his cheek (11:4) and making the vineyards flourish again (1).

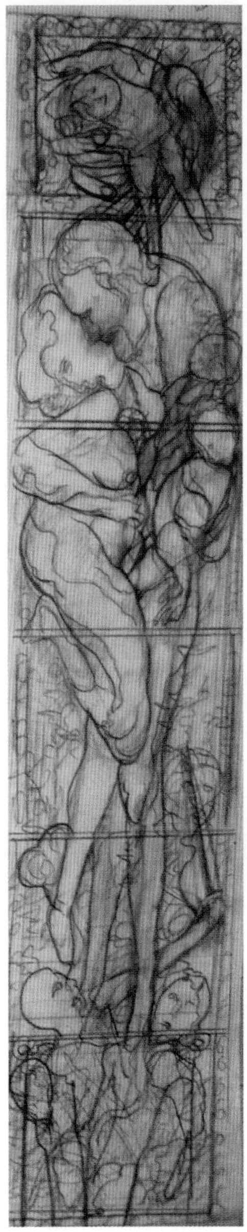

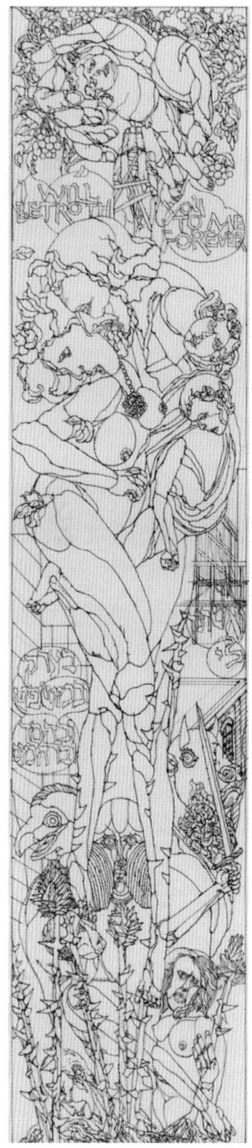

LEFT Sketch for Hosea window. At the top of this sketch, Landau writes the word "Birds." He adds the actual image of a bird to his later drawing (panel 5). From the private collection of Rosa T. Giletti.

RIGHT Drawing for Hosea window. Jacob Landau Collection, Monmouth University Galleries. Courtesy of Monmouth University.

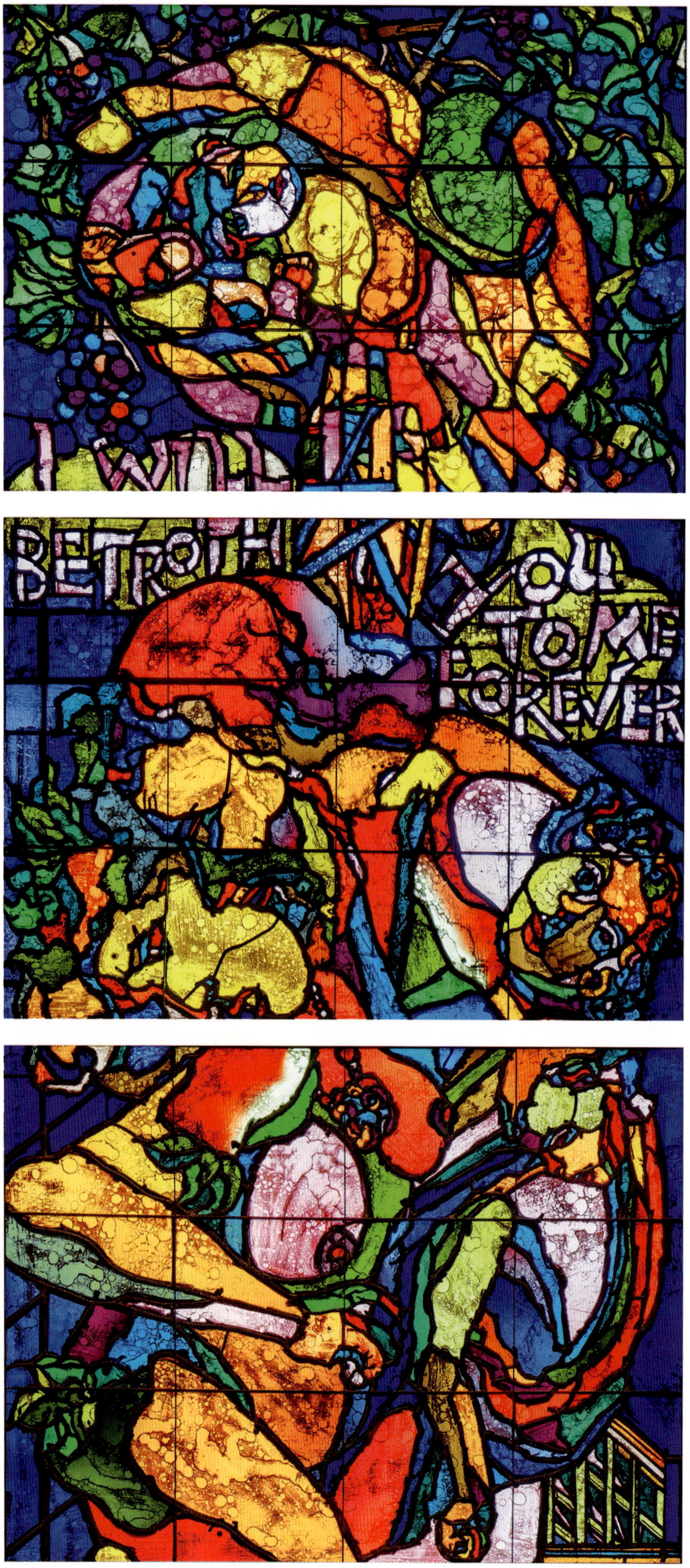
I WILL
BETROTH
YOU
TO ME
FOREVER

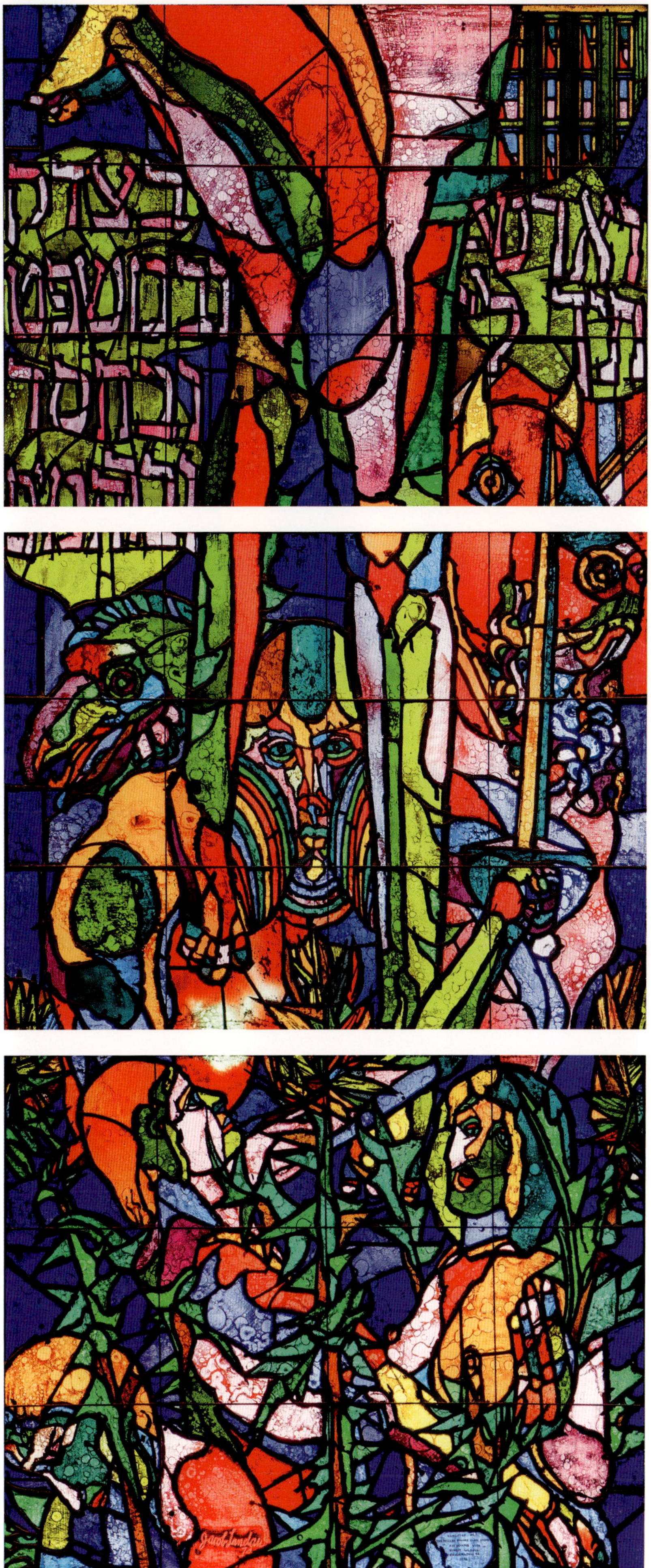

Isaiah

WORDS: (4–5, Eng) The wolf shall dwell with the lamb (11:6); (4–5, Heb) A little child shall lead them (11:6)

FIGURES: (1) a child running to our left in front of a mountain, at its base the top of Isaiah's head; (2) Isaiah's centered head in profile with flames flaring out to the right from his tongue; (1–6) his body extending upward the length of the window from the dead stump at the bottom; (1–2) four heads of Isaiah, the blue one facing right breathing flames (2) behind two in profile, one looking upward and one looking downward, the last just below them to the left facing us; (4) David playing the arteries of the prophet as if they were the strings of a harp and looking upward reverently toward him; (6) face of a dead man upside down below the Star of David lower left

OBJECTS: (1) a cloud above the horizontal rays of the sun over Mount Zion, the Hebrew letters of "Lord" on the Holy Ark in the center of its lower slope; (1–5) sapling tree with fresh foliage; (2) heart with vertical arteries behind, both surrounded by the fresh foliage; (3) arteries with the lion, lamb, and wolf on our left surrounded by foliage; (4–5) word balloon on the left (Eng) and on the right (Heb); (5) foliage, and tree stump below, out of which grows Isaiah's tree-body; (6) dead roots and national flags of Britain, Israel, and the Soviet Union, and a dragon's neck and head emerging from the dead roots, under the Soviet flag

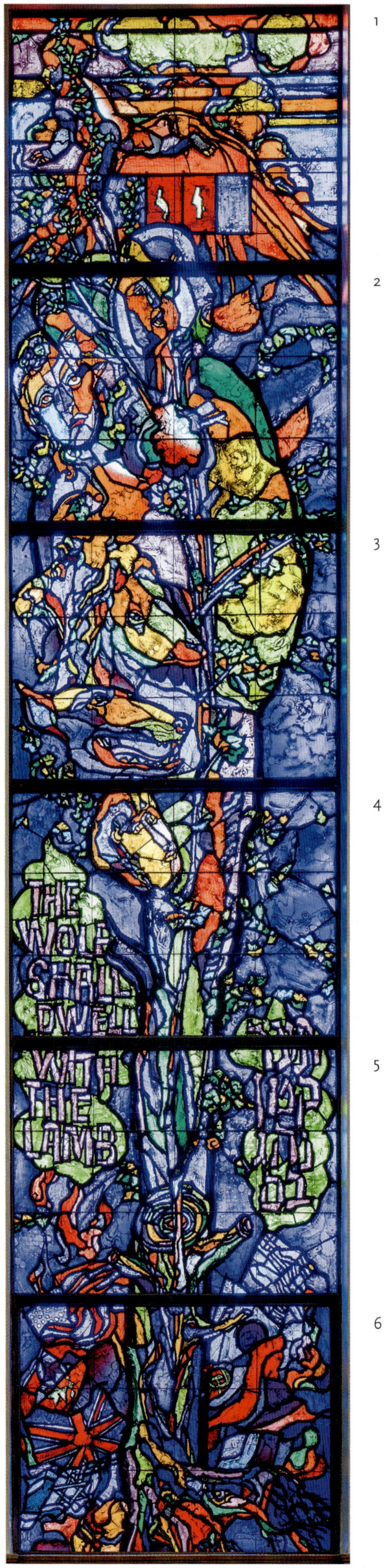

Here we come face to face with the prophet's body, whose circulatory system is a flowering twig that passes through him into the running child on Mount Zion (1). Our eyes move upward with the body from dead-stump dark to living sunlight. We also find ourselves standing before the words of the prophet, "The wolf shall dwell with the lamb" and, in Hebrew, "A little child shall lead them" (4–5), the word balloons filled with the same light as above. These images crystallize Isaiah's hope, even in the face of imminent destruction, for the end of war, the restoration of justice, and the ultimate survival of his people.

To accomplish this, Isaiah's words like fire (2) consume corrupt rulers and foreign enemies (24:21; 30:27–28). And from this arises justice, for the Lord is a God of justice (30:18). Like Amos's and Hosea's God, Isaiah's God does not care about liturgy (1:11), only action. His people must free the oppressed and relieve the poor (1:17; 10:1–2). The rays at the top of the window remind us that all depends on man's actions, which determine whether they are sunrise or sunset, promise or apocalypse.

With the restoration of justice—of Eden, where the lamb lives with the wolf—the tree of knowledge in the Abraham window becomes the tree of life. This is the tree of Jesse, whose line produced King David, and if justice prevails, the tree will flower in the child headed into the future, ensuring the survival of a people.[7]

Unlike Abraham's tree-body of knowledge, which questions the origin of justice, Isaiah's assumes its origin in God. Landau expresses this by the window's astonishing unity centered in the body. This image is a fitting climax to the first wave of windows, as the form and color dissonances of Abraham's body, the clash of legs and arms, are resolved in the single chord of Isaiah's.

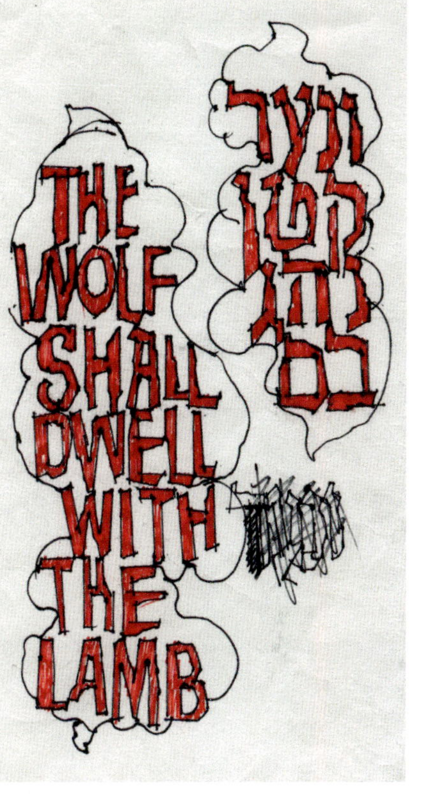

Draft of word balloons for Isaiah. From the private collection of Rosa T. Giletti.

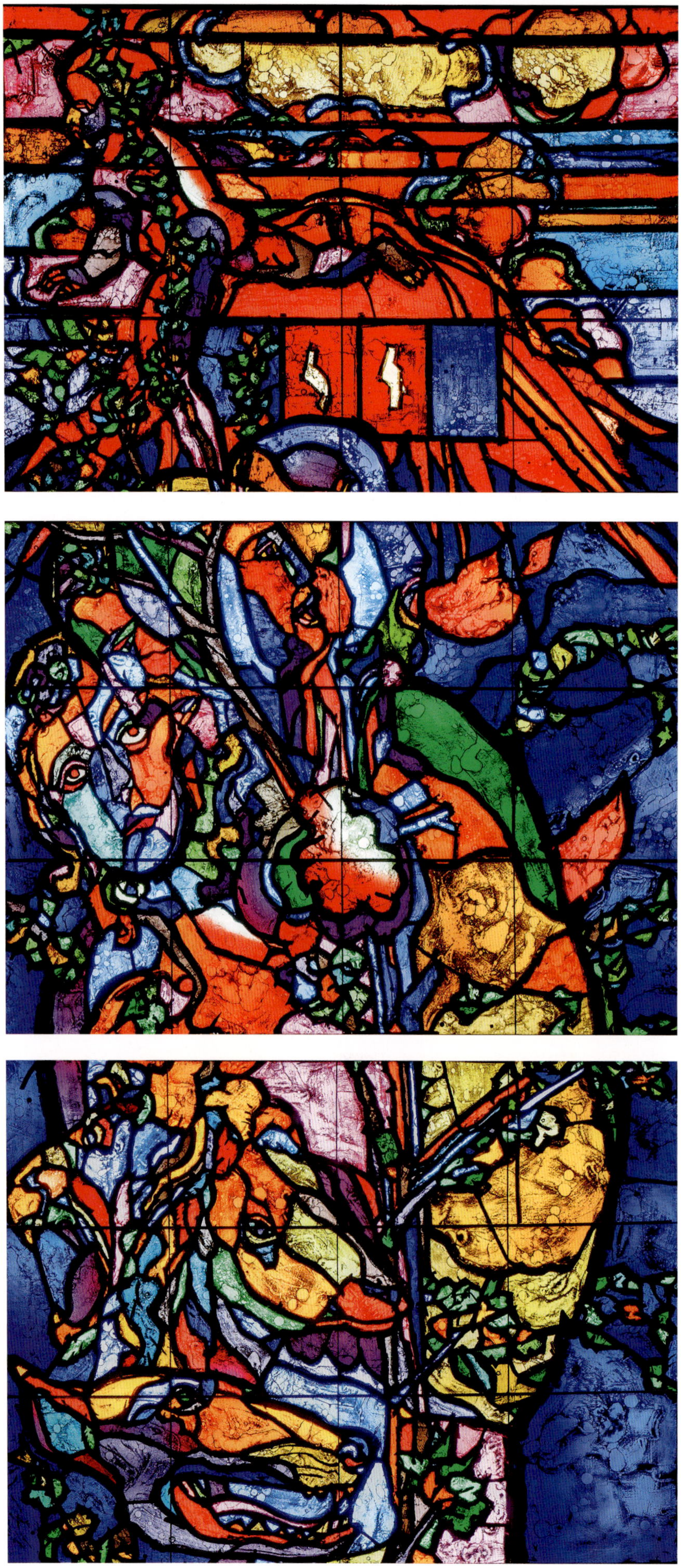

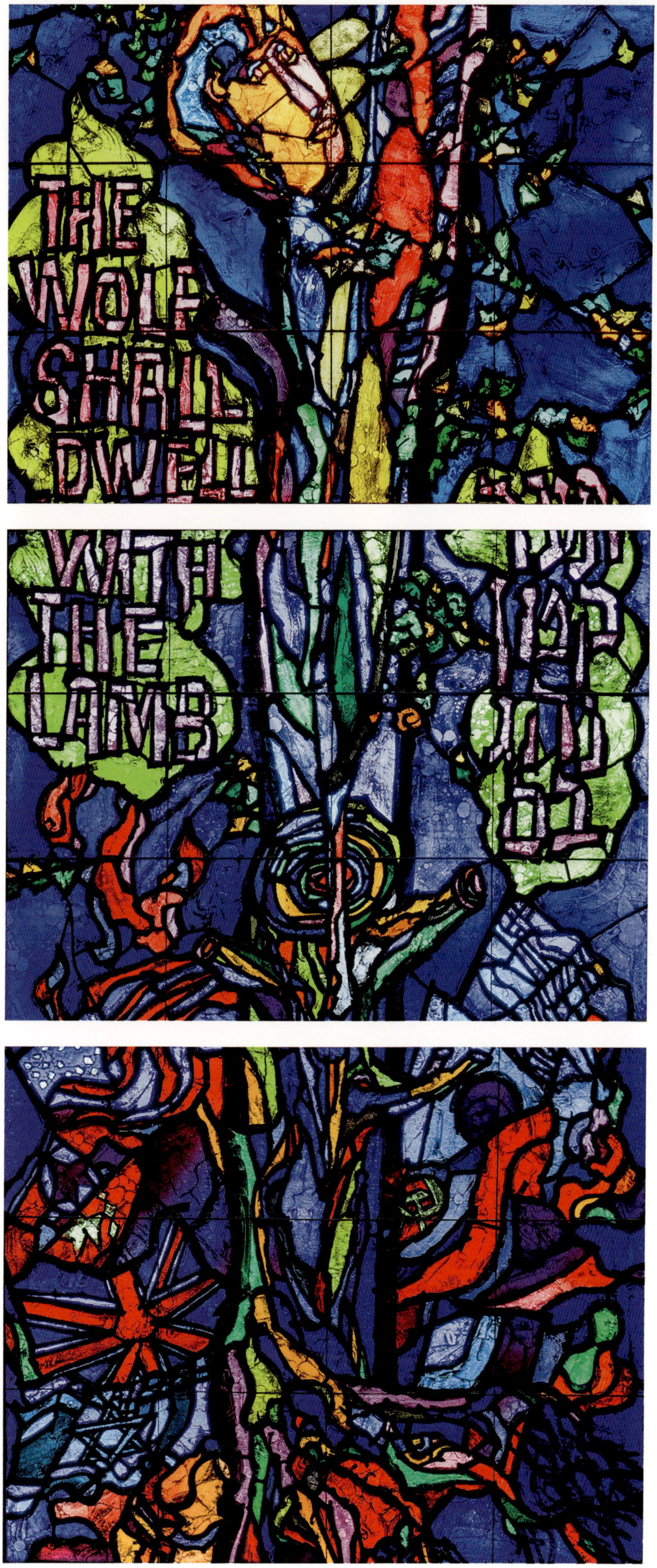
THE
WOLF
SHALL
DWELL
WITH
THE
LAMB

Second wave of windows: Jeremiah to Malachi (right to left). Photo © 2013 Tom Crane Photography.

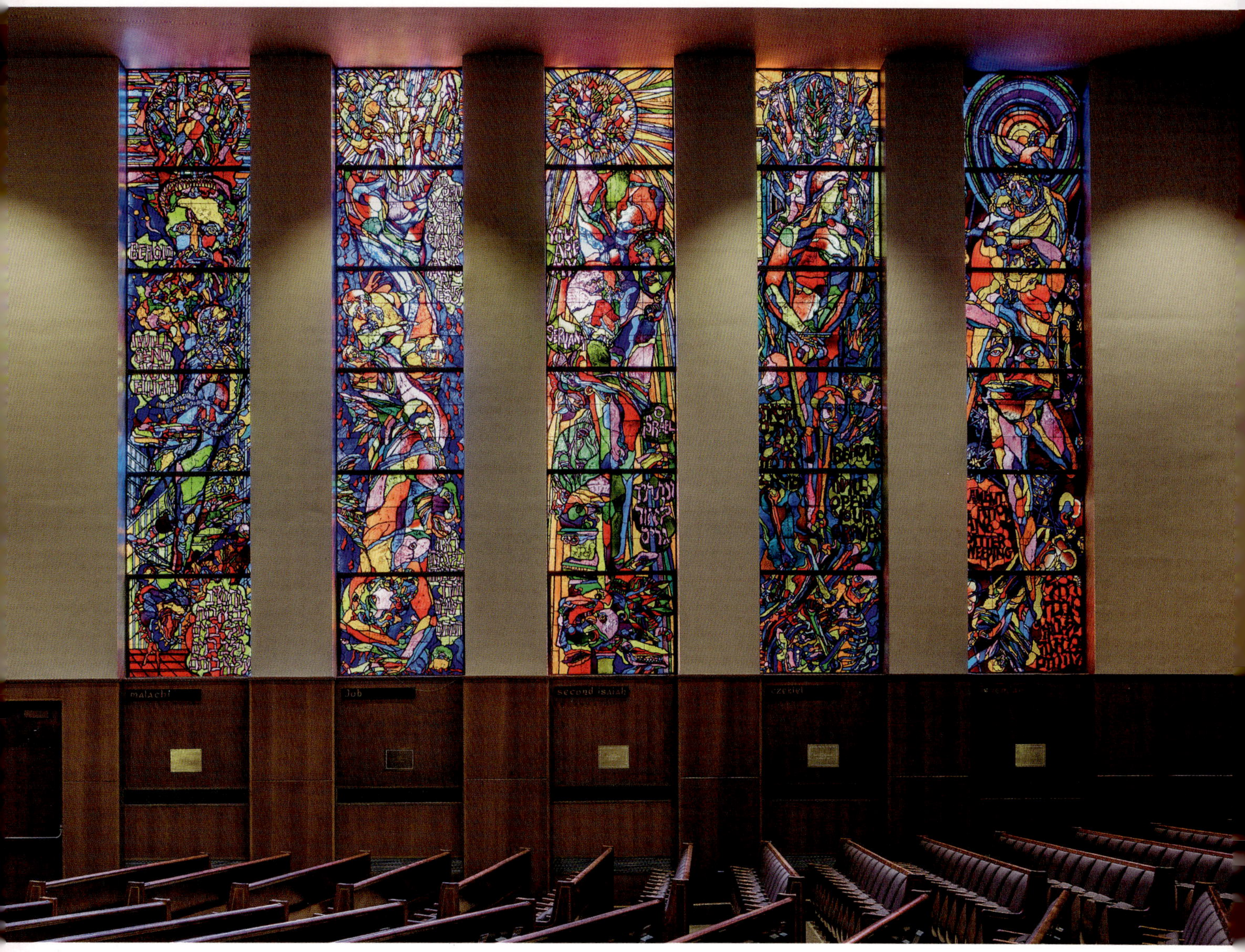
malachi
Job
second isaiah
ezekiel

Jeremiah

WORDS: (5, Eng) Lamentation and bitter weeping (31:15); (6, Heb) Rachel weeping for her children; she refuses to be comforted (31:15)

FIGURES: (1) one of Rachel's children straddling Rachel's shoulder and celebrating with upraised arms; (2) Rachel holding another of her children, and below, Jeremiah peering out from among flames that engulf his head; (3–4) Jeremiah's naked torso, his right arm holding a living head/mask; (3) another of Rachel's children hanging from her lap, with its head to our right facing upward and hand dangling; (4–6) Jeremiah's right leg, which strides toward us, and behind it skeleton-like figures wrapped in burial shrouds, (6) their heads to our lower left and (5) legs stretching upward to our right

OBJECTS: (1) halo enveloping Rachel's child; (2–5) explosions of light; (3–4, Jer 6:27) living mask and to our right a tower; (5) word balloon on the left (Eng) and (6) on the right (Heb); (6) sun-fragment in upper right corner

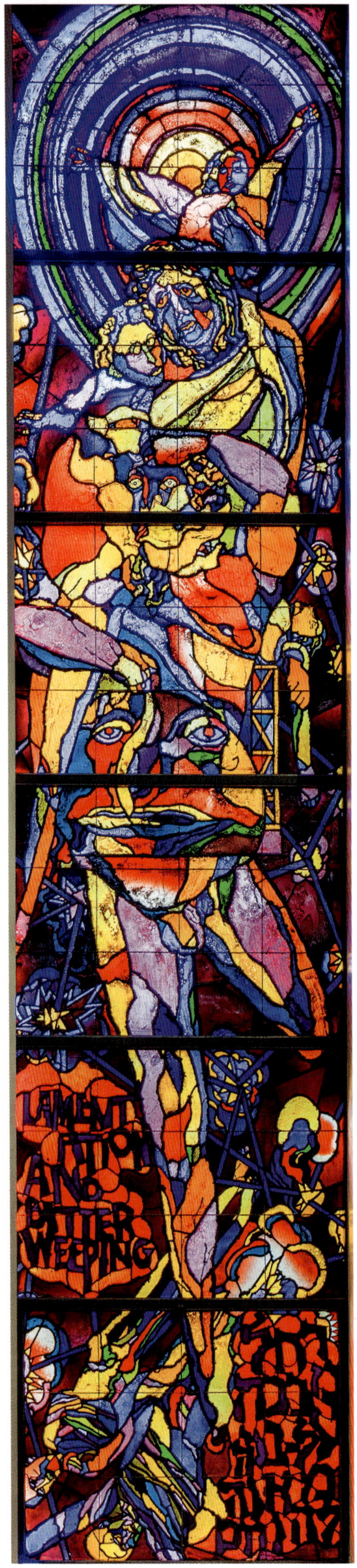

1
2
3
4
5
6

Abraham initiated the first wave of the prophets' quest for justice by challenging God as Lord; Jeremiah launches the second by entering into a conversation with God as person.[8] And this dialog reveals not only Jeremiah's inner wrestling but God's as well (4:19, 14:8–9). Having to pronounce God's "sentence" on the very ones he loved (4:12), Jeremiah's mission, like God's, was both tragic and transcendent. The artist's central images express Jeremiah's ambiguous position as a prophet, hating his role while being faithful to it. This tension of his life as a stranger preaching justice in his own land animates the window.[9]

Reflecting this, Jeremiah's partially obscured head itself is ambiguous. Is the fire from his mouth (2–3) a condemnation of injustice (5:28; 22:13, 17), searing words that threaten to devour the people like wood (5:14)? Or is he immolated by the flames of Israel's injustice pouring onto him?

And we are arrested by the head he carries, its devourer's mouth and scimitar nose (3–4). This is the speckled bird of prey (12:9) that warns his people of their doom if they do not embrace justice. They will become carrion at the hand of invaders in a land of deep darkness (2:31), as evoked by the black background (in contrast to Isaiah's living blue). Or perhaps this is Jeremiah's severed head, as he divorces himself emotionally from his role as prophet.

But the naked Jeremiah striding boldly toward us is the searcher for the true man of justice and righteousness. God has told him to run through the streets of Jerusalem and see if there be anyone who seeks truth (5:1). The great force of the prophet's will and action is expressed by his body's explosive energy, bursting from the artist's carefully ordered composition, diagonal counterpointing diagonal (4–6) and word balloon (Eng) balancing balloon (Heb). The "bitter" lamentations sound from both sides as he strides through the city, casting doubt on Jeremiah's success.

Yet we are given hope. The unambiguous child at the center of the rainbow halo celebrates the future new covenant of God, who will make man the "habitation of justice" (31:23, 31).[10] In this act the first wave of Landau's quest shifts to the second, from God as bearer of justice to man as bearer of justice.'

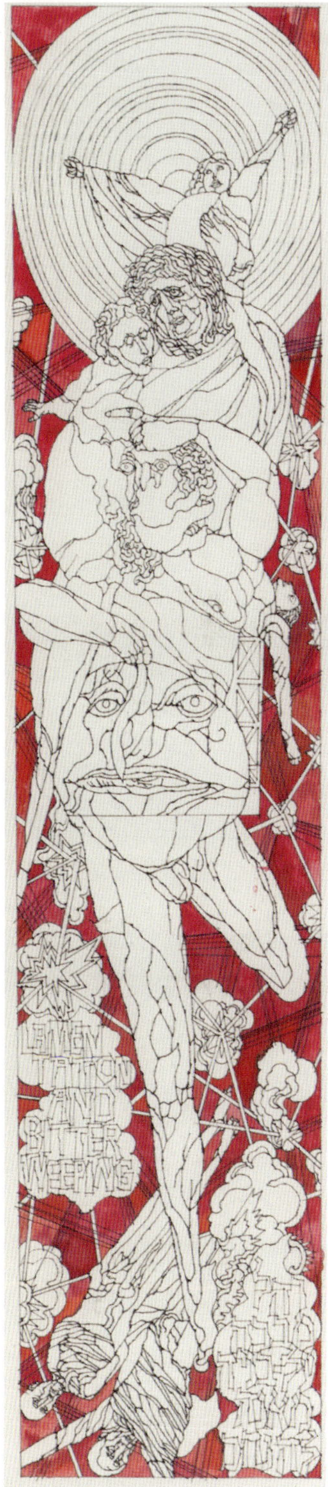

Drawing for Jeremiah. Jacob Landau Collection, Monmouth University Galleries. Courtesy of Monmouth University.

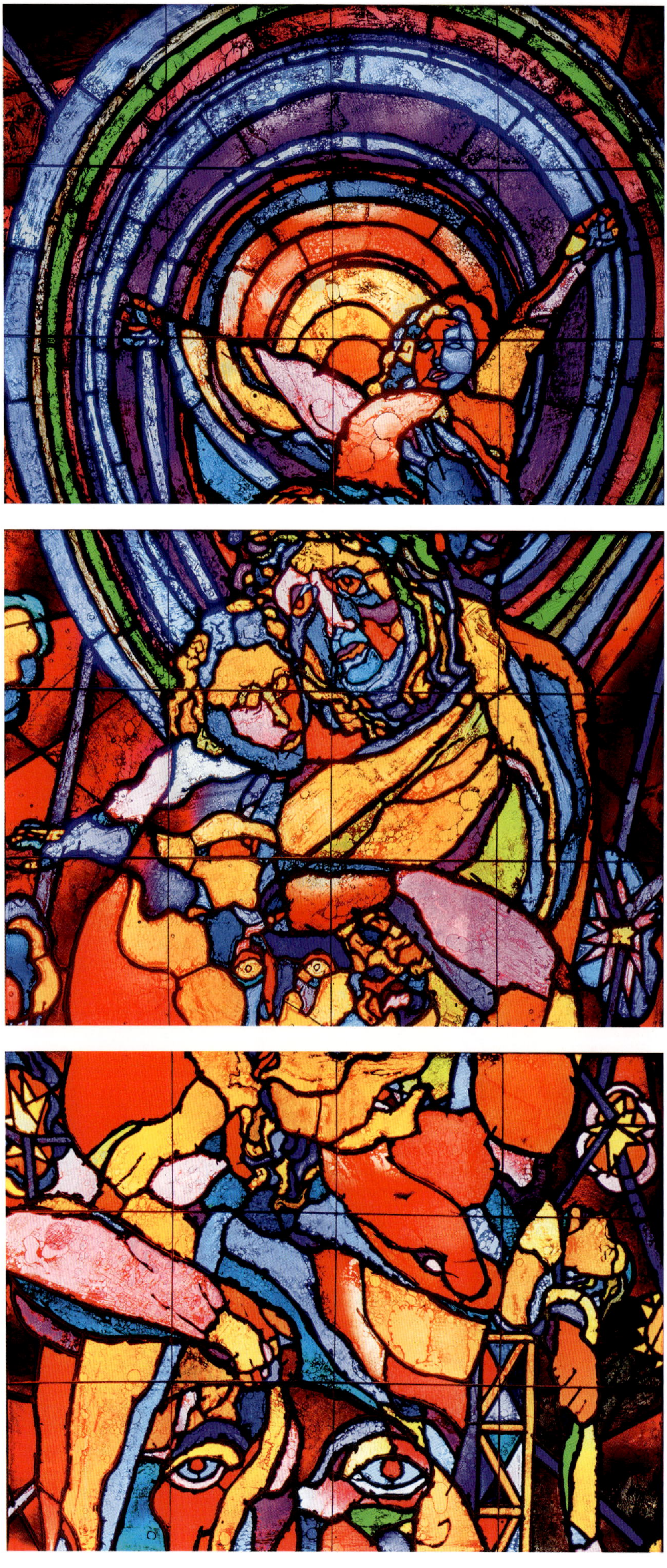

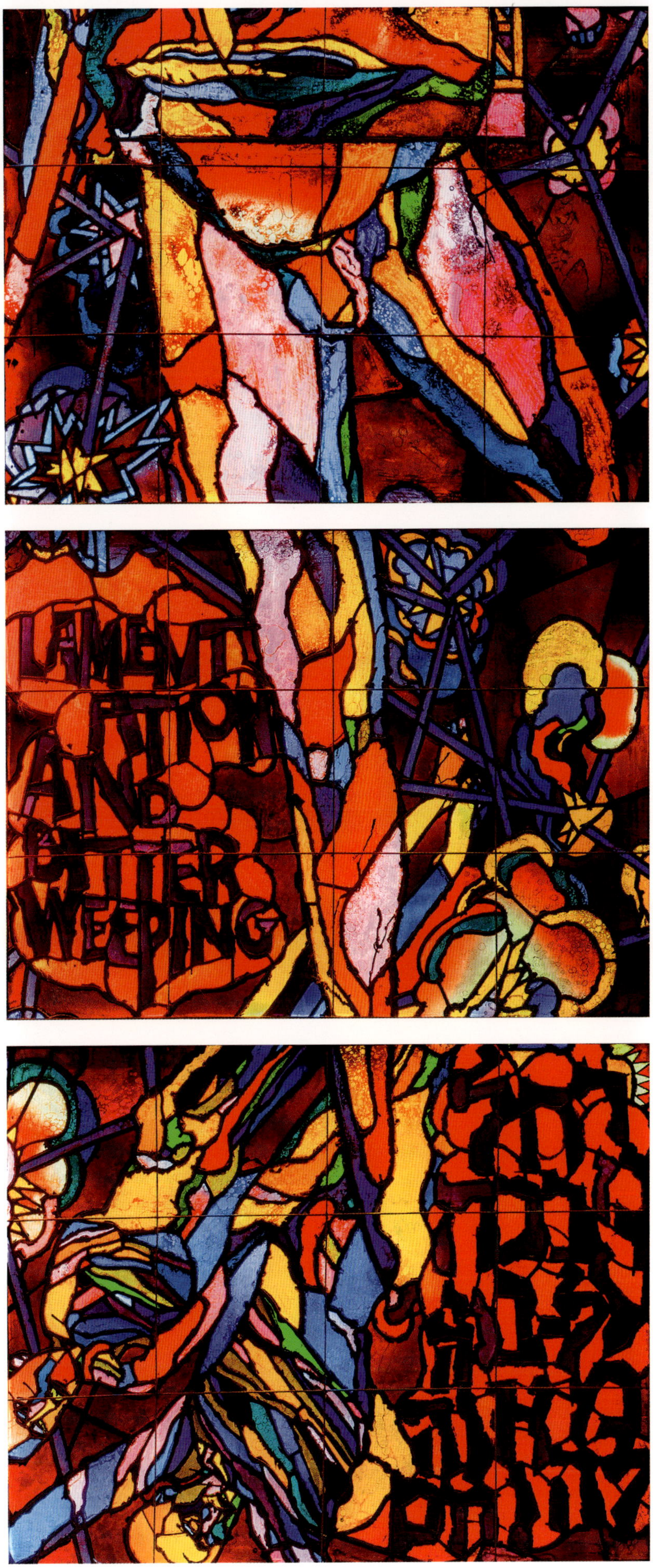
LAMENT
ATION
AND
BITTER
WEEPING

Ezekiel

WORDS: (4–5, Eng) Behold I will open your graves (37:12); (4–5, Heb) I will bring you back to the land of Israel (37:12)

FIGURES: (1) Israelite warrior brandishing a gun in the upper left; the faces of two warriors in profile left and right of center; two other warriors, one in the upper left and one in the upper right; additional warriors, one at the very top right with his head against the arch, and one to the right of the right-hand warrior in profile (total six); and (1) two arms and hands reaching above the temple arch in triumph; (2–5) captive Ezekiel in profile looking to our right, his torso facing us, and (2) a fellow captive on our right; (3) Ezekiel's lower torso and upper thighs with his hands bound together over his genitals; (3) a multicolored, upraised hand on our right of the (4) fellow captive just below with his head on its side, balanced (3–4) by another facing downward on the left, and (4) a corpse-like third in the center facing out

OBJECTS: (1) large prickly pear (sabra plant) in the shape of a tribal war mask or shield in the center, within a temple arch; gun in a warrior's upraised hand, upper left; (2) temple columns flanking Ezekiel; (3–5) green vines or his green entrails flanking him, (4) cords binding his hands; (4–5) word balloon on the left (Heb) and right (Eng); (5) bones rising, bones of Ezekiel's shins and foot exposed; (5–6) skeleton foot and flames in upper left; skull in upper right above a pile of ribs and leg bones

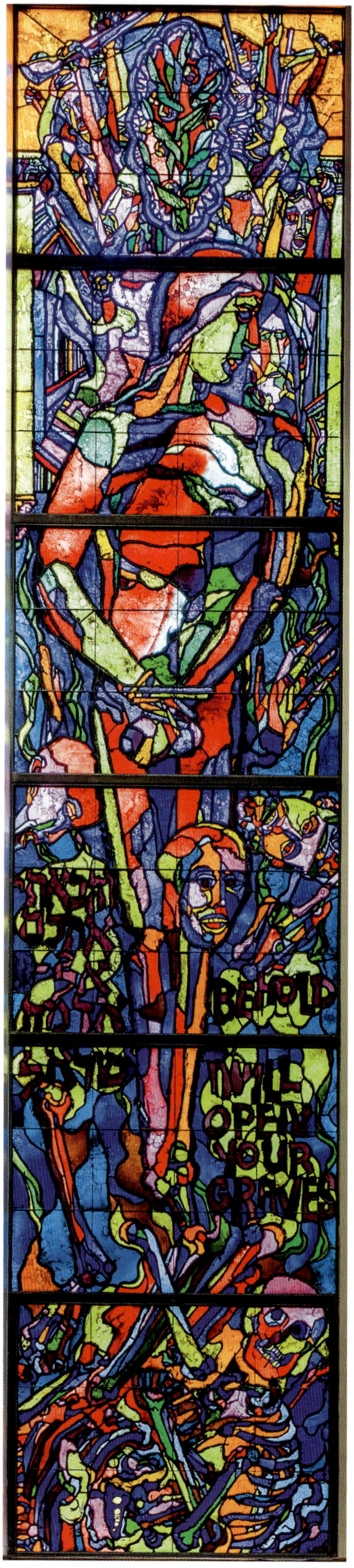

1
2
3
4
5
6

Ezekiel's body is assembling itself from dry bones before our very eyes and becoming the restored temple, as he prophesies. "The prophet becomes the prophecy" here, as Landau says. The window itself is Ezekiel's vision, the restoration from desolation. Though he is bound among his fellow captives in Babylon, his statuesque stance and head tilted slightly downward express his mental peace.[11]

Uniquely still and whole among the other fragmented prophets of the quest, who are caught in motion, Ezekiel's calm, self-contained body commands our attention. The artist captures him in a moment of vision, his gaze turned inward, in contrast to the captive beside him, his tongue sticking to the roof of his mouth (3:26).

Ezekiel, by his visions and symbolic actions such as eating a scroll (3:1) and sketching the city of Jerusalem on a tile (4:1), makes himself the drama in contrast to the House of Israel (6:11), and this is the prophet that the artist presents to us. This image undergirds Ezekiel's turning away from his fellow prophets' focus on collective responsibility. He is focused instead on individual responsibility.

When God announces the coming disaster for the righteous and the wicked alike, Ezekiel does not hold the community responsible so much as the individual. He entreats each of the princes of Israel to cease their violence and execute justice (45:9). After the Lord's all-encompassing announcement, this is the justice possible to believe in, an individual obligation.[12]

Landau depicts Ezekiel with his huge heart covering his entire chest, echoing the Lord's promise to replace each person's "stony heart" with a "heart of flesh" (36:26). In Landau's vision of Ezekiel assembling himself, the prophet's bones take on more and more flesh as we move from bottom to top, as dark blue gloom gives way in a transformative rising motion to the vibrant gold of promise, from bones to flesh to restored temple and liberation.

Midway in this motion the artist prominently places a long-fingered hand, half flesh and half bone. This aspiring hand is a dramatic image of hope next to Ezekiel's cropped hands.[13] The sabra plant (prickly pear) at the top (Ezek 28:24), the symbol of Israel's army, signals that this hope is well founded. The Lord has opened the graves of these warriors and they are retaking their land from the Babylonians; individually, like the princes of Israel, they are restoring justice as Ezekiel promised.

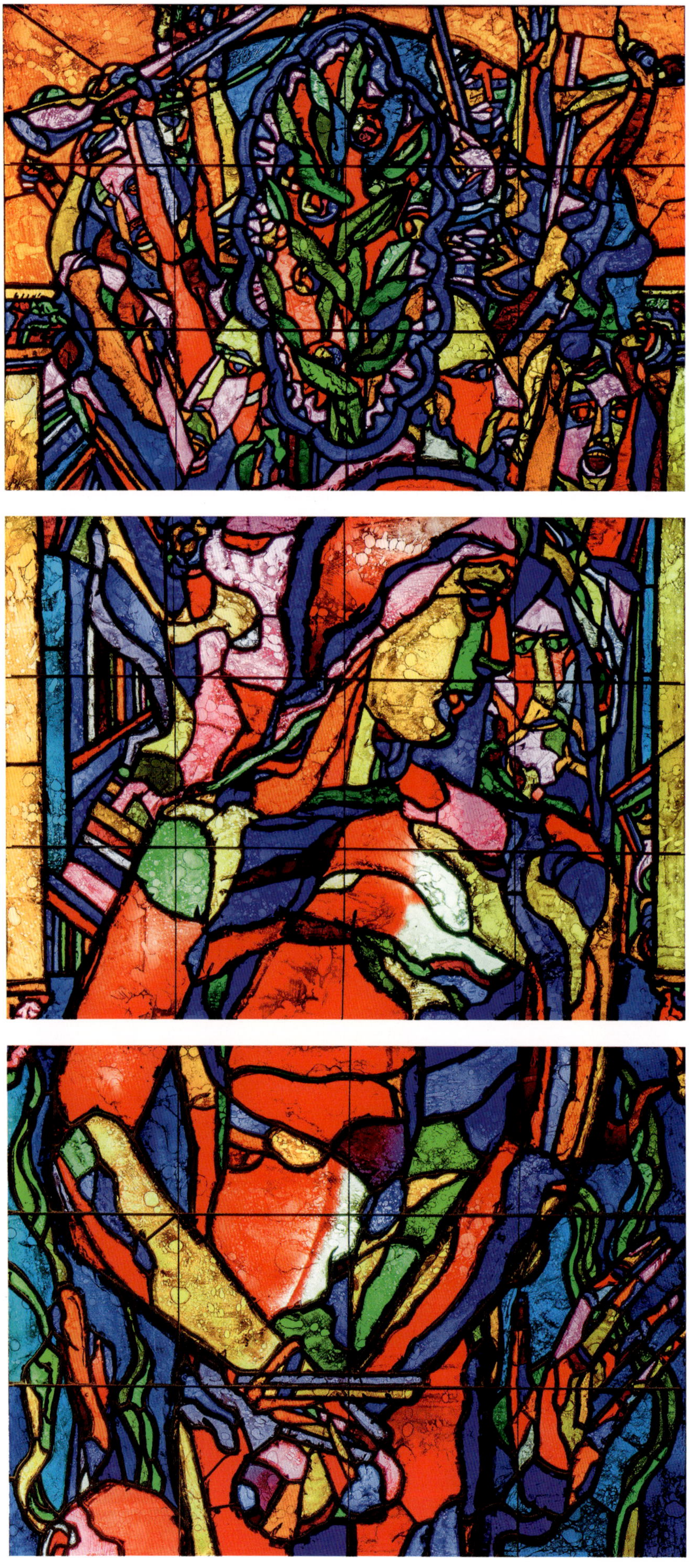

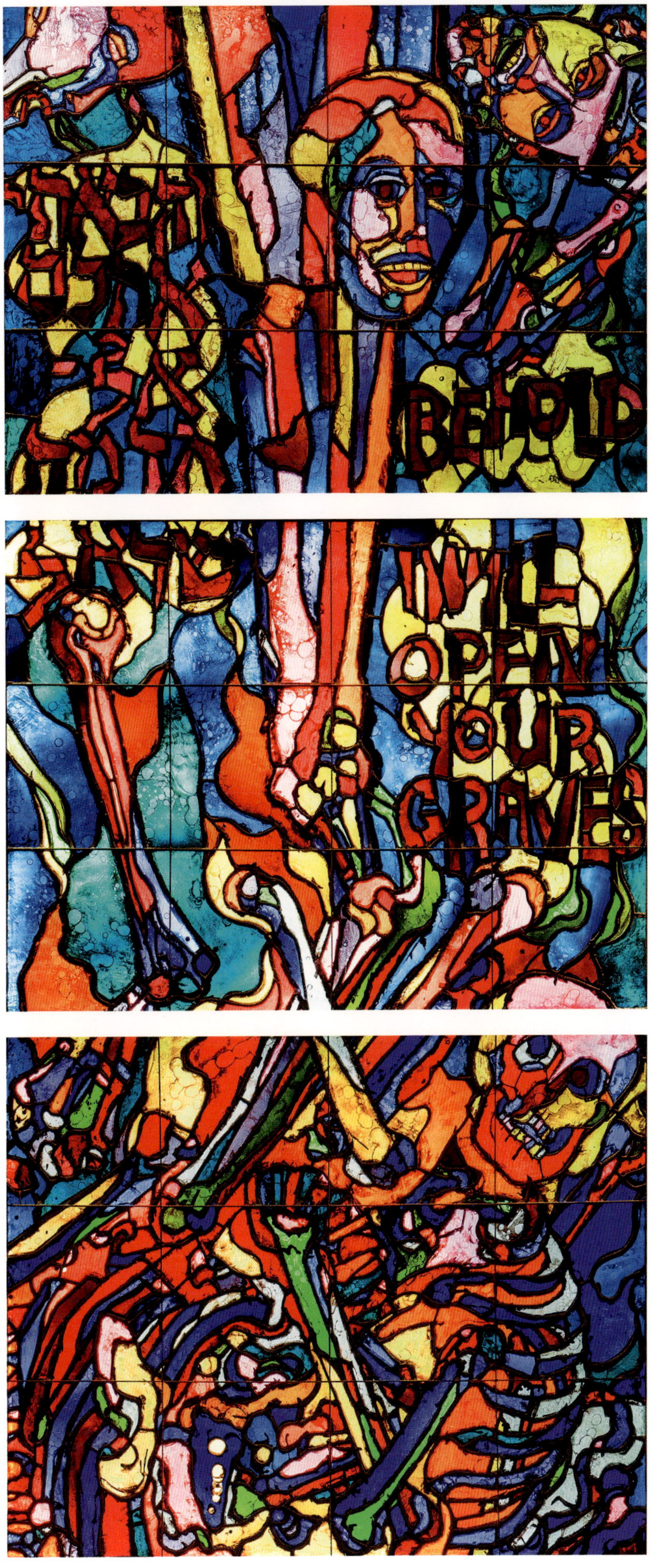
BEHOLD
I WILL
OPEN
YOUR
GRAVES

Second Isaiah

WORDS: (2–4, Eng) You are my servant O Israel (49:3); (5, Heb) I will make you a light unto the nations (49:6)

FIGURES: (2–3) torso of the headless Second Isaiah with (2) heart displayed right of center; (2–3) blind severed female head facing us; (3) blind male head in profile, bent down toward the word balloon; (4–5) Isaiah's overlapping legs center; and upside down head of a human sacrifice on our left

OBJECTS: (1) flower resembling a great circular sun, raised by the stump of Isaiah's arm, with (1–6) rays bursting from it down through the entire window; (2–4, Eng) word balloons; (3–4) flowers with colored stems girding Isaiah's thighs and connecting the "Servant" and "O Israel" word balloons, which lighten as they near the sun; (5) capital of a pillar on our left supporting a severed arm tilted up to the right; word balloon on right (Heb) with a serpent's head under it; (6) false god, with vacant eyes and tongue lolling from the mouth lower left, and pagan bird-idols

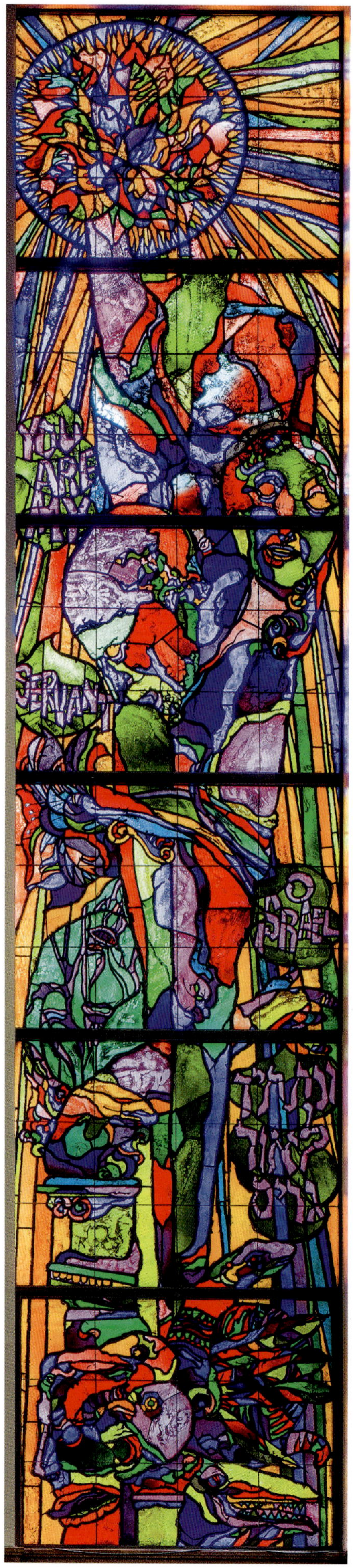

1
2
3
4
5
6

The "suffering servant" stands before us mutilated and dismembered (52:14). By the time of Second Isaiah, what Ezekiel feared had come to pass with the fall of Jerusalem. Traditionally, the prophets considered themselves simply servants of the Lord, but Second Isaiah assumed the role of a suffering servant. As the Second Isaiah window dramatizes, this servant is not Israel the nation as a whole, but an individual—a person whom the Lord, admitting to some remorse, has given over to the merciless Babylonians (47:6).

For it was hardly a case of justice that Israel's agony was Babylon's glory. Isaiah's mission, in part, was to imbue the people's suffering with meaning. And he does so, comparing them to the pains heralding a birth. Isaiah becomes the suffering servant because suffering is necessary for the new-born Jerusalem to triumph and "go forth as brightness" (62:1). Landau symbolizes this triumph by the glorious sun blooming from the body that opens up with the rising window.

To achieve his mission, Isaiah speaking for the Lord attempts to turn his people—who, he reminds us, are first and last servants of the Lord—toward justice (56:1). And the suffering Isaiah that we witness here reminds us that the Lord depends on humankind, on each individual, to effect justice. He will not rest until through them justice is established on earth (42:1–4; 54:8).

In the radiant flower-sun held high by a dismembered prophet, its rainbow rays of promise filling all space, Landau expresses Isaiah's unshakable belief that every individual is precious and will be redeemed. He has confidence that all will devote themselves to justice, that the blind man who bends his head to the flowers girding Isaiah (3) and repeats the word "servant" will open his eyes to its real meaning as one who brings justice to the nations (42:1). The isolation of the word balloon, a change from Landau's preliminary drawing (fig. 53), suggests that humanity will ultimately know that it is only by their individual acts, not by human sacrifice (4–5) or bird-idol worship (6), that justice will prevail.

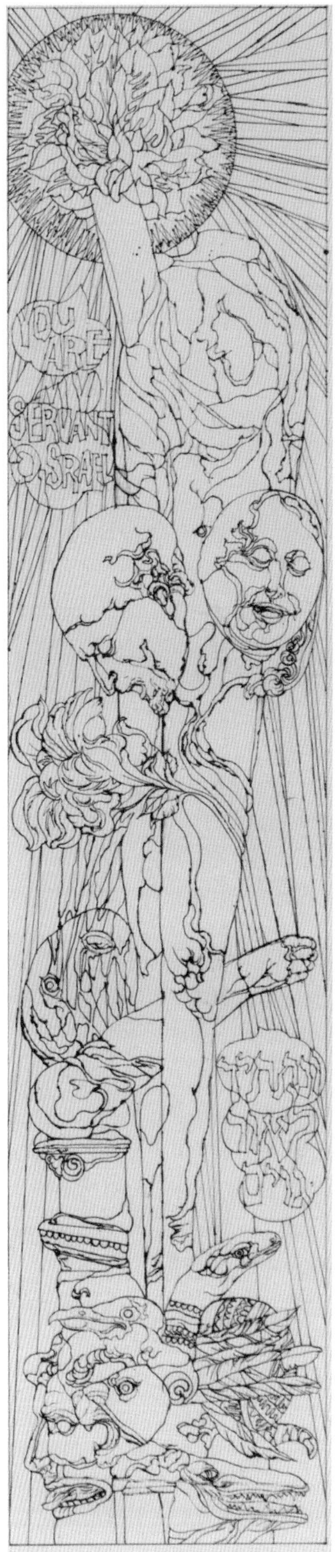

Landau's preliminary drawing does not separate the "Servant" and "O Israel" word balloons. Jacob Landau Collection, Monmouth University Galleries. Courtesy of Monmouth University.

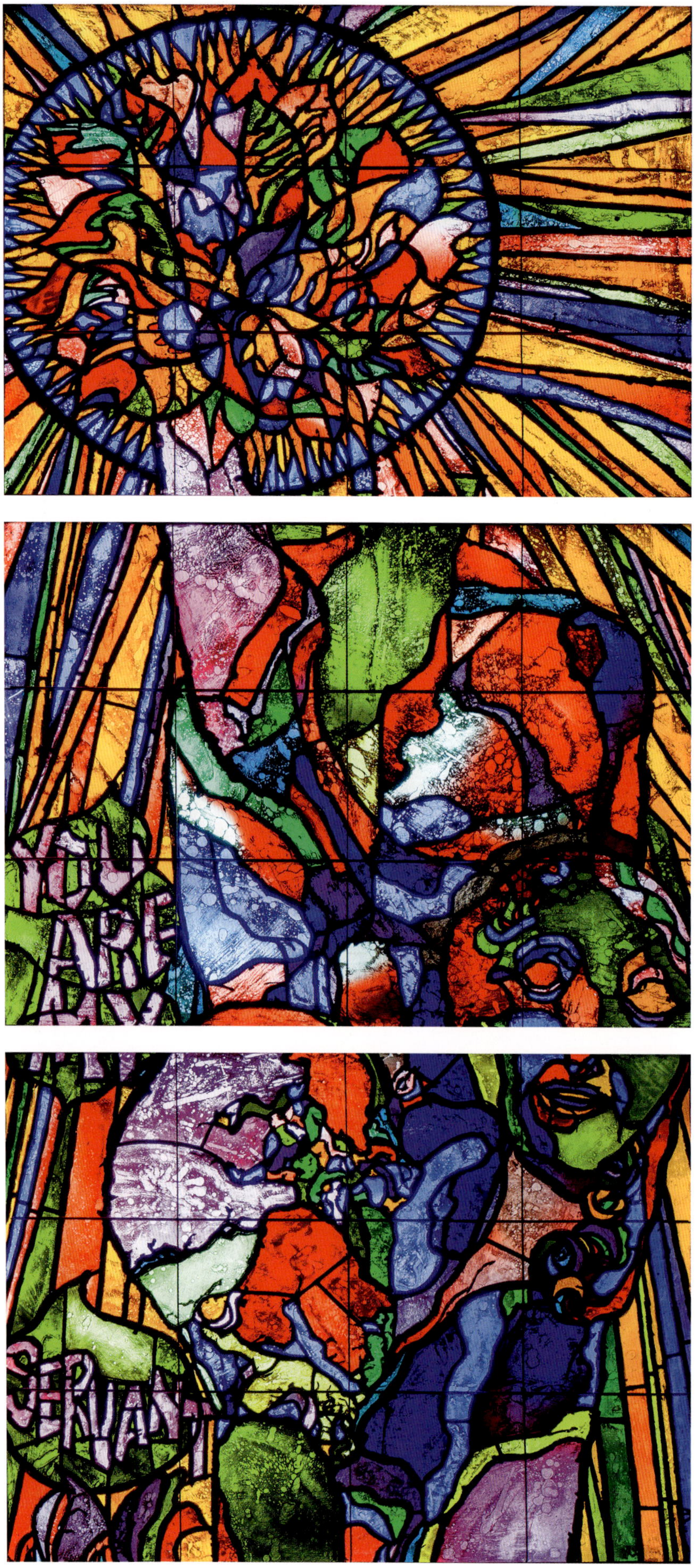
YOU
ARE
SERVANT

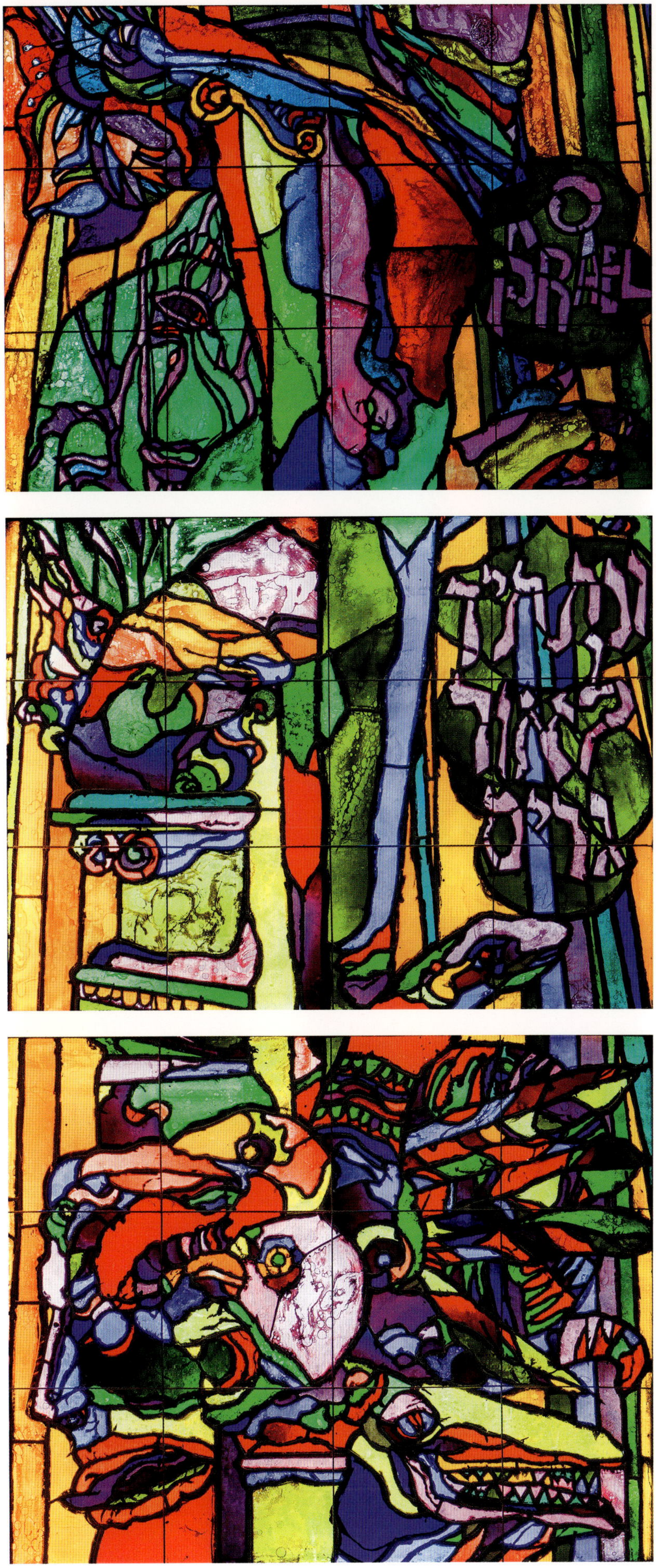

Job

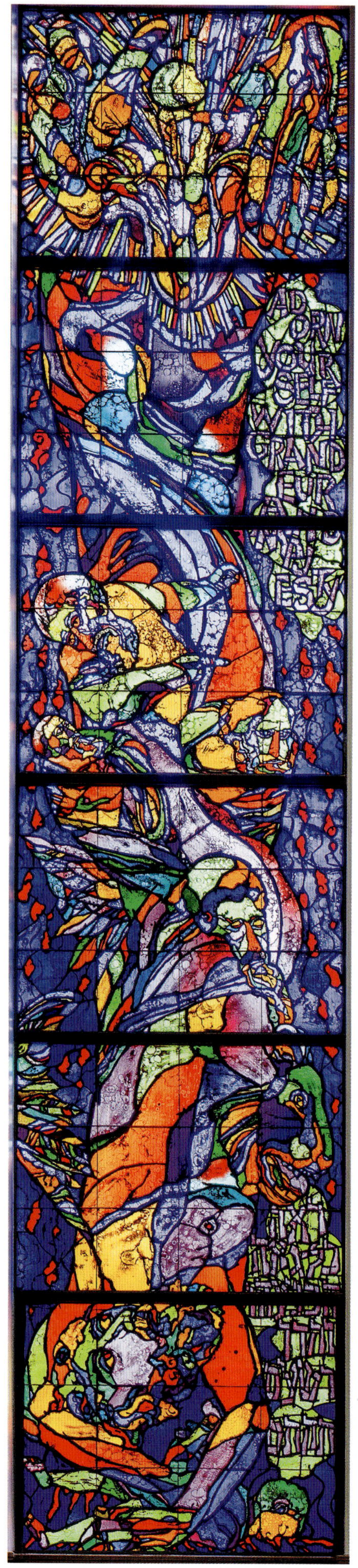

WORDS: (2–3, Eng) Adorn yourself with grandeur and majesty (40:10); (5–6, Heb) Look on everyone that is proud, and bring him low; and tread down the wicked in their place (40:12)

FIGURES: (1) two large hands holding a flower that cradles a naked babe, its back to us; (2–3) woman's body rising; (3) one of the comforters of Job, bending his head down to our left and pointing at the English word balloon and red droplets to the right, with heads of two other comforters below; (4) the fourth comforter with his head turned toward us, feathers at his back; (5) Job's body falling headfirst, his heart an open wound beside the head of a fierce lion and (6) one hand on his dead child, who is lying face down horizontally across the bottom of the panel

OBJECTS: (1) large flower; (1–6) red droplets against the background; (2–3, Eng) word balloon; (5) lion with open mouth on the right, bird's plumage opposite; (5–6, Heb) word balloon

The curves of a voluptuous woman catch our eye first, her head a blossoming lotus flower (40:21–22) from which emerges a naked babe. The lotus stem's curve flows upward, from a falling male body into an ascending female body that resembles an Indian goddess, in the upper half of the window. They are the same body: Job rises as a transcendent woman after his tragic suffering as a man. Puzzling.

Through this image of a falling and rising androgynous body, Landau expresses Job's dilemma: he expects God to do justice but finds that God expects him to do justice and to become, as Job does in this window, the figure of "wisdom," personified in Job (28:20–21) and explicitly identified as a woman in a passage dear to the artist (Prov 1:20).[14]

Enduring gratuitous suffering, sanctioned by a God who hunted him down like a lion (10:16) and tore out his heart (5), Job asks him, Why do the wicked live? (21:7). But out of the whirlwind, God in turn asks Job, Why do you question me? (38:5–41). In effect, God says that his creation of the world is sufficient, having nothing to do with justice.[15]

Justice in the world is thus up to us. God invites Job to "adorn" himself with "grandeur," entreating him to accept this awesome responsibility on earth—doing justice by treading down the wicked (40:12). He must rise in majesty to his "grand" task (this syllable emphasized by its isolation in its balloon), embodying wisdom itself and giving birth to a just future. He must gain his independence as man, becoming fully human, by acting in the world to effect justice (40:14). Thus Landau concludes, God will be more just as we become more just.[16]

Abraham calls God to account but assumes that he is just, while Job concludes that justice is not God's business, but man's. With this recognition, Abraham's tree of the knowledge of good and evil becomes the tree (lotus plant) of life (Jewish and Hindu). Job must take his own life in his hands and go about the business of destroying the wicked, transforming the red droplets of blood falling from victims into seeds of new life rising (13:14; 21:8).

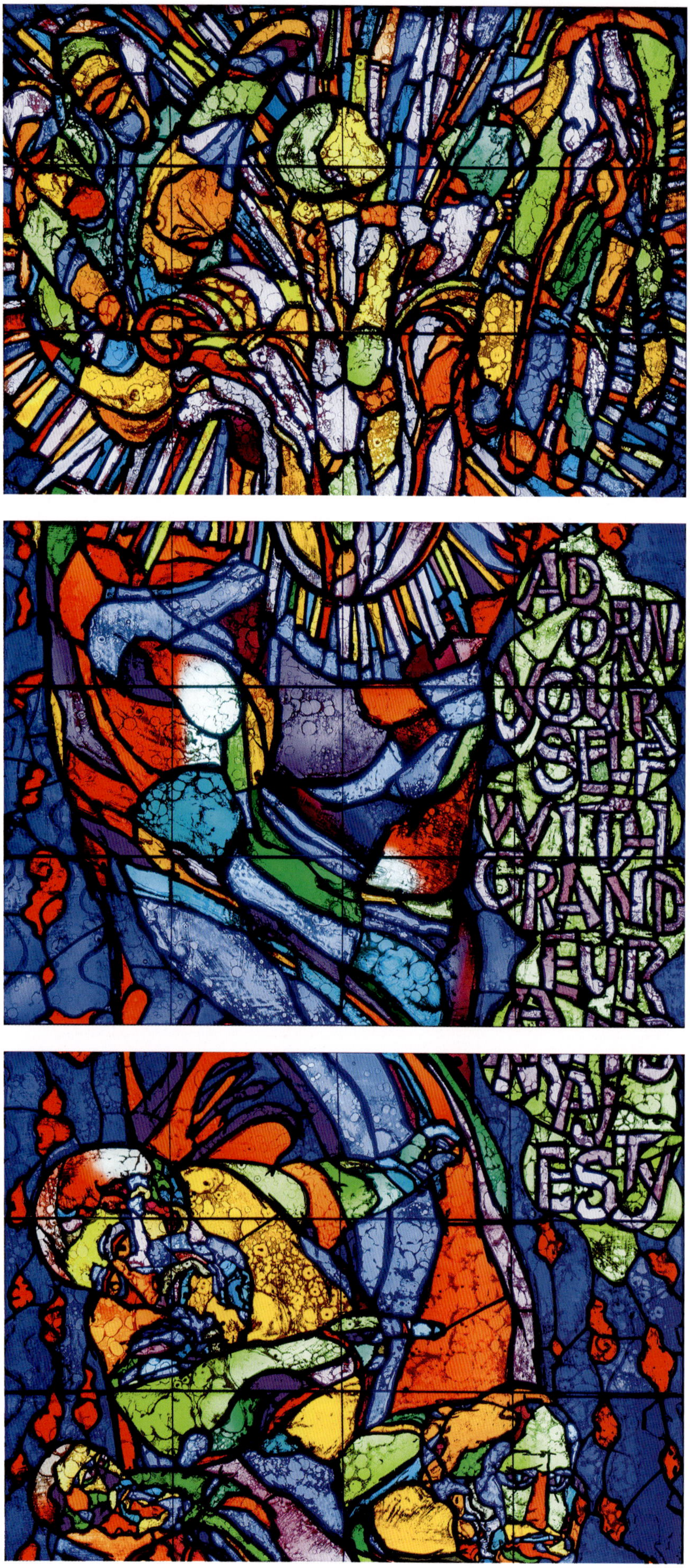
AD
ORN
YOUR
SELF
WITH
GRAND
EUR

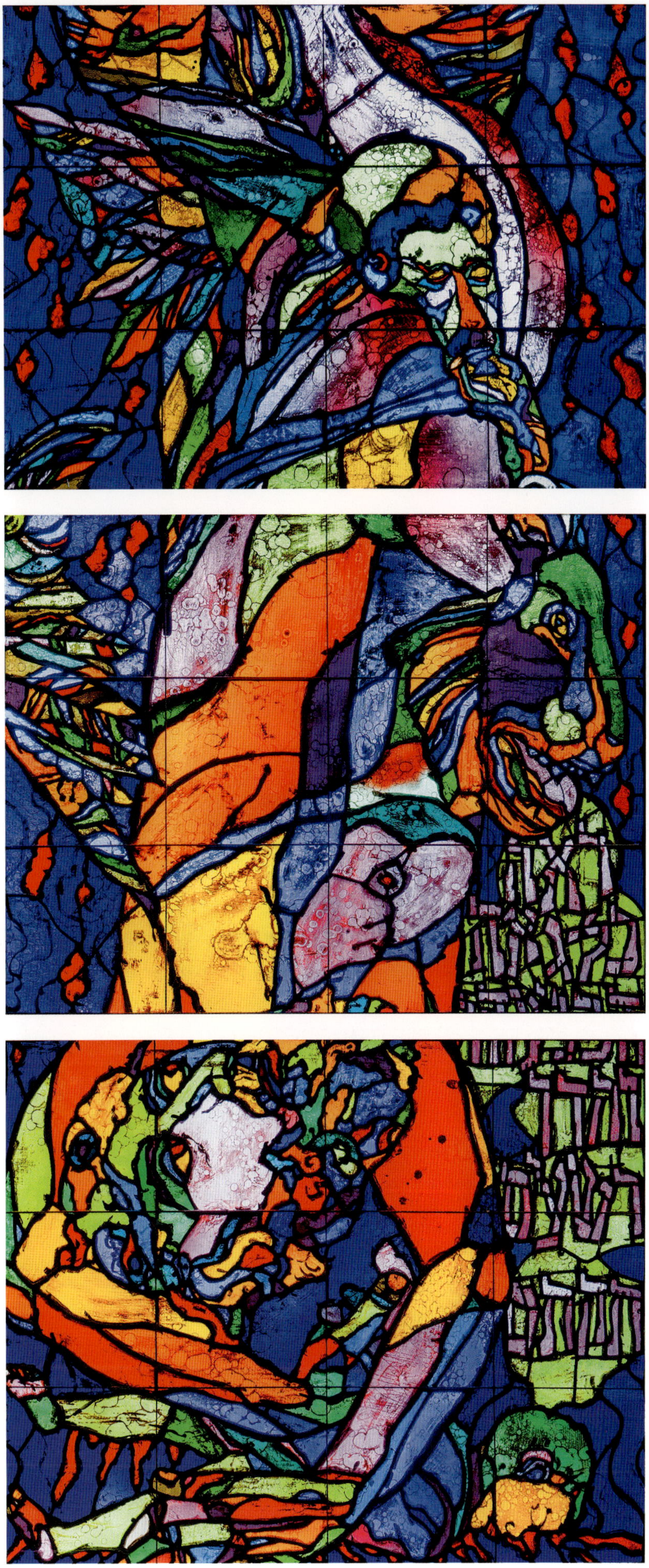

Malachi

WORDS*:* (2–4, Eng) Behold I will send you Elijah (4:5); (6, Heb) He will turn the hearts of fathers to children, and the hearts of children to their father (4:6)

FIGURES*:* (1) child welcoming the viewer with one hand and raising the other hand in triumph against backdrop of a large open hand; (2) Malachi staring straight at us; (3–5) the daughter of a strange god, her breast cups exaggerated, looking downward to the left, a futuristic helmeted man (like an astronaut or diver) with a tube at his mouth and his eyes on us running toward our right, his legs extending below; (4) a head in profile on the right breathing from a tube; (5) a soldier with his back to us falling diagonally, legs extended upward to the right, his hands reaching down to the left holding a gun, and two other soldiers on the lower right with arms out

OBJECTS*:* (1–2) elaborate headgear extending from Malachi's head, horizontal rainbow colors in the background; (2–6) curtain wall in the background; (2, Eng) first word balloon, "Behold"; (3–4, Eng) second, "I will send You Elijah"; (4) artificial heart in the helmeted man's boxlike chest, with tubes and arteries coming from behind it, one tube out to the right, the other to the left; (4) severed, floating hand to the left speaking the words in the balloon above; (5) gun in soldier's hands; (6) head of lion in profile to the left, eyeing the viewer, speaking the words in the balloon on our right (Heb)

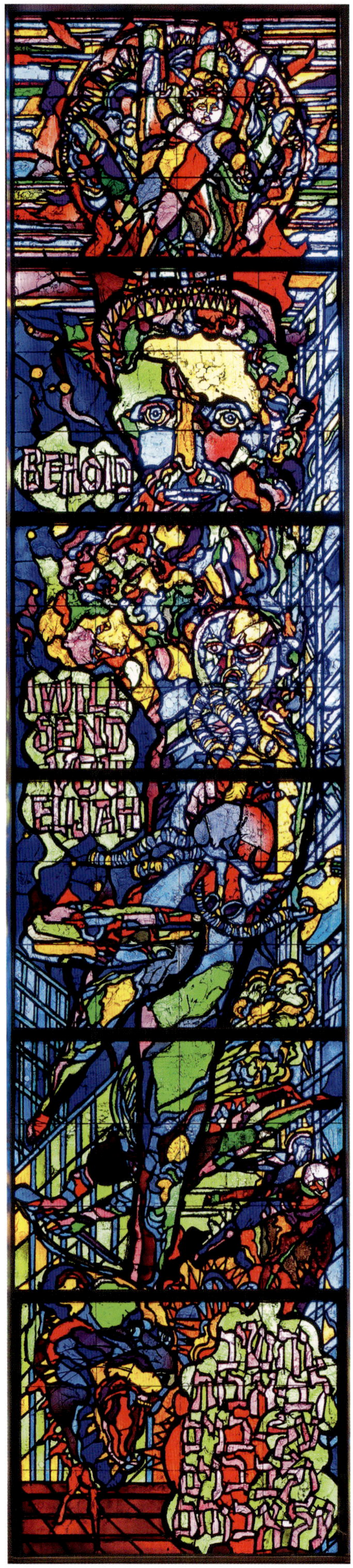

1
2
3
4
5
6

The penetrating stare of the prophet arrests us in our tracks. Malachi demands our attention—"Behold"—and gets it, promising future deliverance from the "great and terrible day" to come when the wicked will be burned up (4:1). But, ironically, because Judah has betrayed Israel by marrying "the daughter of a strange god" (2:11), Malachi seeks not to deliver justice but to defer it.

And the prophet he promises is not the scientifically improved, futuristic technological man at his side with a determined stare that is promised by our age. No, the prophet promised by the hand (4) offering human justice, the only justice that God will ultimately accept (1:10, 13; 2:13), is the lion (6) we met earlier in Amos. All must now take this lion seriously, the "voice of the fierce lion" not broken (Job 4:10) but hunting us down (Job 10:16) in order to "turn the hearts of the fathers to children" and vice versa (Mal 4:6; word balloon, Heb).

We witness here the artist's unease about the future, his hope for reconciliation and peace but his despair for the next generation. Malachi's elaborate headgear, which binds him to the child, can be either the "Sun of righteousness" (4:2) or a mushroom cloud (fig. 60).[17] Fittingly, it is not the "science fiction super hero" but the lion of justice who promises reconciliation and, as we know from Amos, possesses the will to make justice prevail.[18]

We cannot escape Malachi's eyes, piercing us from the past, or the superhero's eyes, looking to the future and holding us responsible as individuals. Man's quest for justice has worn down even the Lord. He is "weary" of questions like "Where is the God of justice" (2:17 [JPS]), but the prophets persist.[19] Hearing Job, we know we bear responsibility for present justice (36:17; 37:23); hearing Malachi, we know we are responsible with Elijah's help for future justice as well.

Yet like the jarringly dissonant colors and fragmented forms of Malachi's face, the very nature of justice unsettles us. We are left with no choice but to embark on our own quest, deciding what justice demands. We can choose to believe that injustice must be defeated in the present (Abraham–Job), to embrace hope and faith in a just future (Elijah–Malachi), or both.

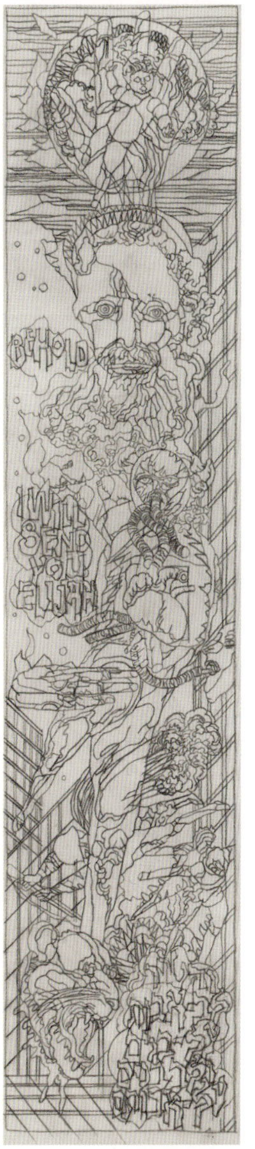

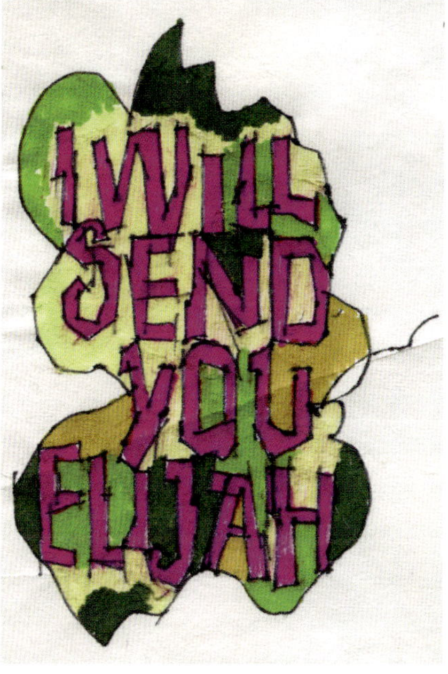

TOP Landau's change from this drawing unites Malachi's radiant and crowned head with the triumphant child as a "sunburst" (panels 1 and 2). This suggests the reconciliation of father and son, a hope dear to the artist, but also strengthens the suggestion of it as a "mushroom cloud," all hope gone. Photo © 2013 Tom Crane Photography.

BOTTOM Draft of word balloon for Malachi. From the private collection of Rosa T. Giletti.

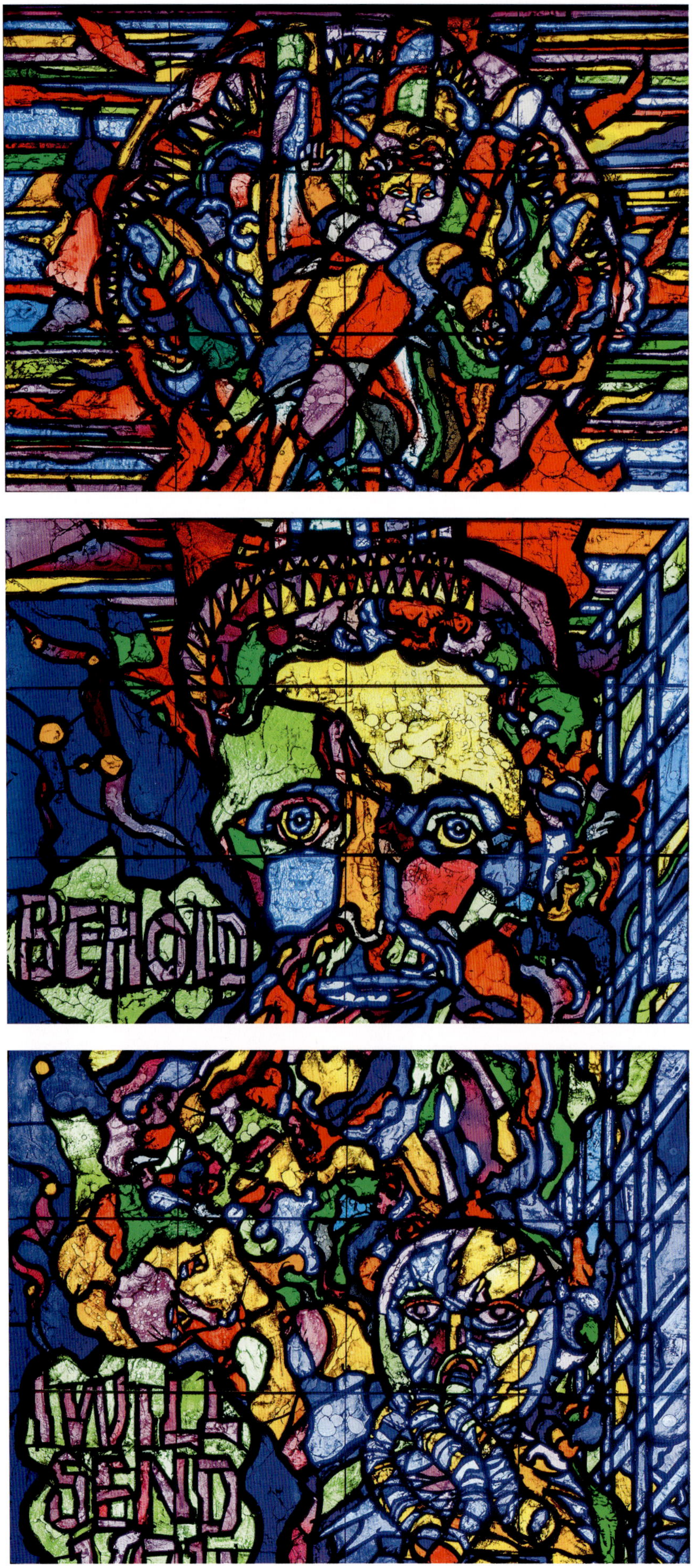
BEHOLD
I WILL
SEND

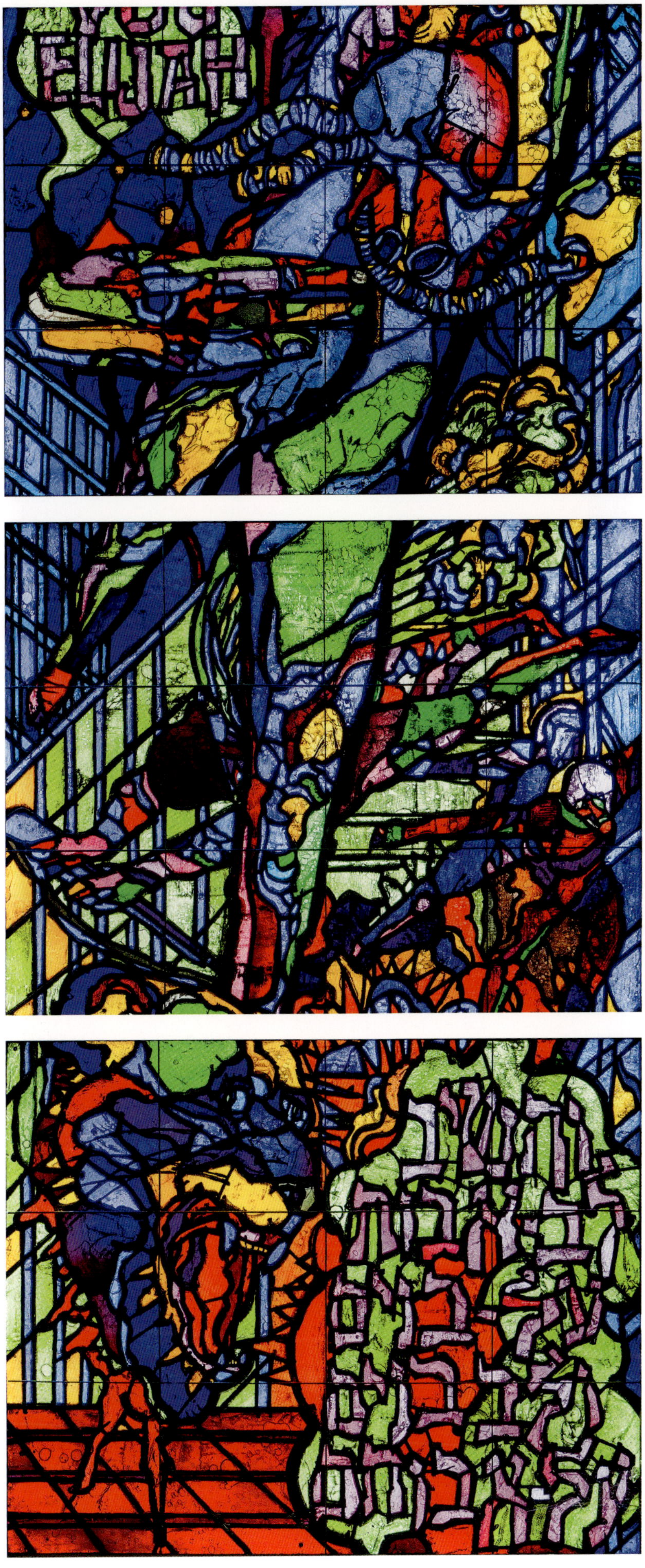
ELIJAH

Reflections

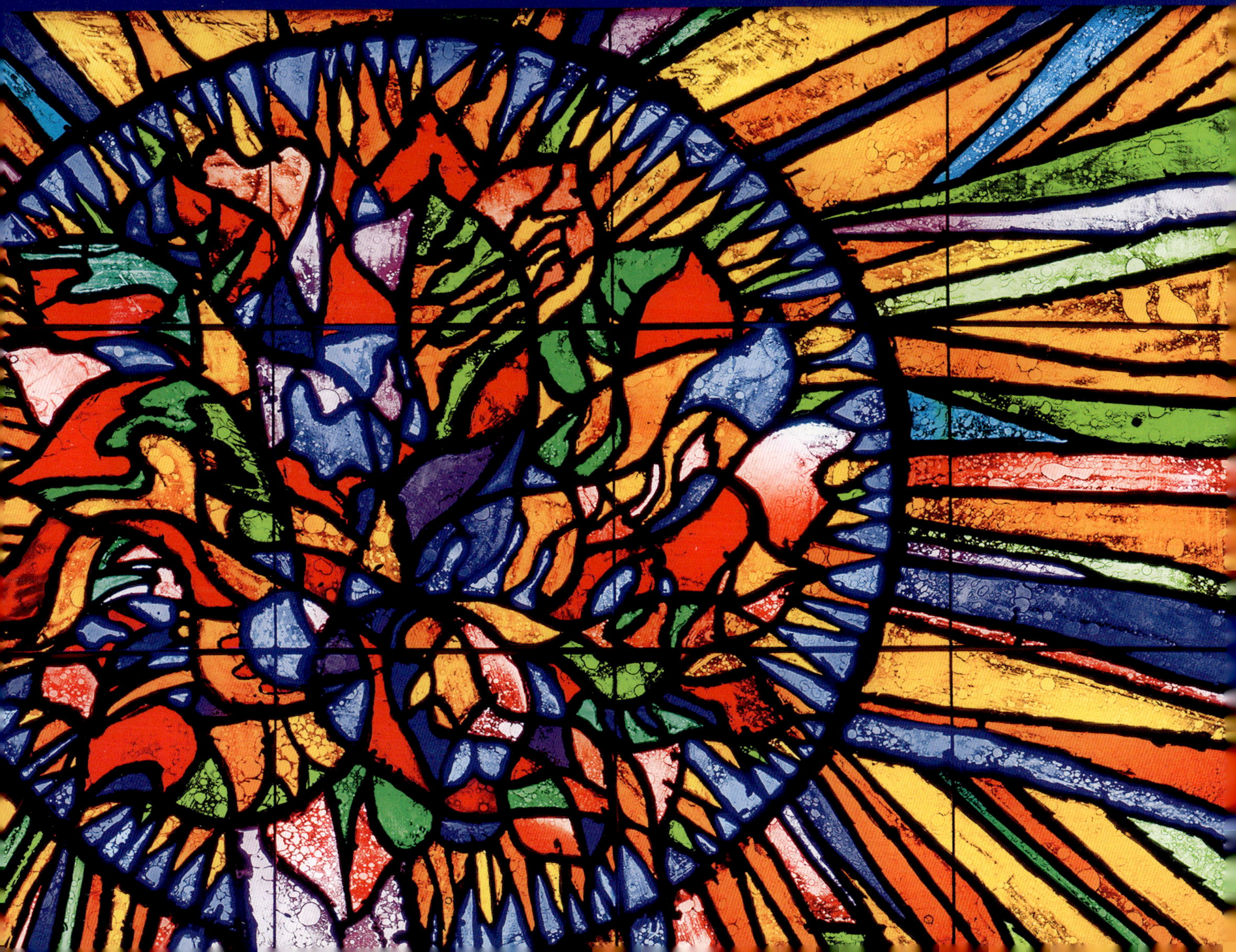

Introduction

Reflections as Midrash

Alicia Suskin Ostriker

Throughout the history of the Diaspora, Jewish imagination and Jewish creativity have flowed through midrash—stories based on biblical texts, composed not for a narrow audience of scholars but for an entire community. After World War II and into our own time, there has been an explosion of midrash in America, reimagining our inherited scriptures, elaborating them, unpacking them, seeking and finding new truths, fresh ways of understanding—sometimes critical, always passionately engaged.

Midrash can take the form not only of writing but of music, dance, drama, film—and of course visual art. Jacob Landau's windows are a brilliant example of midrashic creativity, combining intensity of passion in the explosions of color with intensity of moral utterance in the quotations, even to the extent of inspiring others to creative response. It is thrilling to read these varied reflections, no two identical, each one alive with personal insight into the power, beauty, and meaning of Jacob Landau's achievement.

The multiplicity of these short essays is a true reflection of the complexity of the windows. The windows speak to every viewer differently, and this is as it should be. As the scholar Gerald Bruns has written, "If the text does not apply to us it is an empty text . . . we take the text in relation to ourselves, understanding ourselves in its light, even as our situation throws its light upon the text, allowing it to disclose itself differently, perhaps in unheard-of ways."[1]

An Appreciation

Susan Bockius

It had been years since I last viewed these windows. On that previous occasion I was leading a group tour of Philadelphia-area stained glass. This time I was here simply to view, absorb, respond, and hopefully find words.

What impressed me first, on that quiet day as I sat alone in the sanctuary, was the warmth and joy of the windows taken together. Pinks and yellows, in large swaths, seemed to abound. These sweeps were set off by intense activity areas in which patterns climbed, twisted, and periodically exploded with complexity. Just as one could be washed by the warmth, one could get lost in the detail: text, faces, symbols were created in rich color and pattern that rewarded examination.

I was struck by the strong "descent" in these ten tall openings. A compressed mass at the top diffused or reached or meandered downward. It is a deliberately instructive motif, I believe: God is reaching down to Man; illumination is radiating into life.

The words in these powerful windows both challenge and connect us: "Will you indeed destroy the righteous with the wicked?" asks the Abraham window; "Behold, I will send you Elijah," declares the Malachi window; and "I have found you," says the Elijah window. The power of the declaration upends the usual to disclose new meaning.

These are windows with which to mark one's life; to discover in awe, in celebration, in sorrow, the overarching meaning that is religion's gift.

Fragments of Light and Life

Cassie Brand

When you process a person's archive, you systematically sift through the pieces of paper that document their life. After a while, you start to notice how their handwriting changes when they rush, how they organize letters from their good friends, or how ruthlessly they edit their own work.

This is how it was for me and Jacob Landau. I never had the chance to meet him, but at times, I felt I knew him better than I knew some of my friends. I found myself sitting on the floor of the Drew University library, surrounded by boxes, stealing moments to learn more about this man through his correspondence, sketches, notes, typescripts, and amazing works of art. I learned about his passion for community, his interactions with his family, and his work to foster future generations of artists. I was engrossed, often frustrated when the documents left the story unfinished. Through his archive, I watched his style develop from the age of seventeen, following as it became more abstract, and I cheered when he found his own entirely unique style. It is this style, exemplified in his design for *The Prophetic Quest*, that we can all immediately recognize.

The stained glass windows at the Korn Memorial Sanctuary of Reform Congregation Keneseth Israel bring his work to life in a way I had never previously experienced. At first glance, the windows are an explosion of color. Landau's fragmented style, however, allows for his design to contain a myriad of pieces that come into focus only through careful contemplation of the work. Landau intertwines multiple narrative elements in a single pane, bringing stories to life through strategically placed colors and design. Hidden details invite people to meditate on the windows, giving them the ability to find new elements with each view as they contemplate the simultaneous suffering and hope that the windows portray.

Fragments of glass come together to form *The Prophetic Quest*, just as fragments of papers come together to form Landau's life. Each invites you to take a closer look, to find hidden truths, and to let the fragments illuminate the story.

An Afternoon with the Landau Windows

Arthur J. Dewey

If you come here alone in the late afternoon be prepared
to take off your shoes
as the afternoon sun sets
the windows on fire
and secures the invisible congregation
you will get lost in each elongated frame
wondering how long-lost Kristallnacht fragments
coalesce here in this unexpected
dance of light

begin from the left
read Abraham's worried face
and a question from another argument
(will justice be devoured with the wicked)
as his knife hovers behind Isaac

till your eye catches the sun-dazed wheels
of a chariot lifting Elijah
over the falling heads of bulls and prophets
the saddened eyes of a blue-faced queen

only to be jangled once more by a lion's head
mouthing the words of Amos
blistering at noise religion makes
when it forgets the one
calling out to slaves

then you will be ravished
by a lush bouquet filtering Hosea's
tortured life
the ever returning
promise to a whore

and hushed by the vision of a fiercely colored wolf
in the middle of two phlegmatic lambs

and if you turn to the right
a human figure floats beneath the spheres
above a red-eyed madonna clutching
an uncertain child
your eye follows down
over a beleaguered head
and half a harlequin torso vibrating
only lamentation

then the bound and broken one looks
into the open graves
as skulls and bones
are startled into
the grand cacophony
of life

and under a disc of flaming tongues
with faces inchoate and green
Israel hears the call to repair
a shattered world

but soon is admonished
even as Job jawed with
his comforters plus one
not to get too high and mighty

but hear what Malachi promised
Elijah returning
with a headdress
crowned with a child
declaring the fullness of time

and in the late afternoon
as the sun sets
the windows grow dark
you focus now on the ark
and the words to be read
and realize how Hebrew
is haunting
crowded with memory
for every beginning
starts with “Let there be light”

Stained Windows

Danna Nolan Fewell

Relentless bursts of outrageous beauty
and unspeakable brokenness.
Color, color
exploding everywhere
dazzling,
confounding,
wounding the eyes,
giving shape to quandary,
trauma,
the pain of voicing truths
of infidelity, injury, and injustice.

Rosenzweig would have said,
Landau's art "structures suffering,"
teaching us to bear it,
"to overcome without forgetting."
Each window
an act of kaleidoscopic repair.

Windows past force us to remember:
A god who sometimes destroys
the innocent with the guilty.
Communities in wreckage.
Individuals, families
facing the end of history.
Jeremiah's life of lament.
Ezekiel's valley of bones.
Job's devastation.
Suffering deserved

and lives swallowed up for nothing.
Those who spoke out
and those who were silenced.

We remember.

Windows future flicker
hope, purpose, courage:
We are still here.

In spite of fracture and fragmentation,
we are still here
catching the light
penetrating the walls,
light beckoning beyond,
taking on the colors of story:

A quest.

Prismic splinters coalescing,
demanding coherence—our coherence—
calling us to stir,
step out,
step forward
through the shards:
To espouse divinity,
to walk through fire,
to be a light to the nations,
to become the heralds of peace and healing
for whom the world still waits.

Beyond Decorative

Samuel D. Gruber

Jacob Landau's stained glass windows are the artistic highlight of Keneseth Israel. They enliven a substantial but otherwise unremarkable space. At first glance, the windows appear only decorative. They slash the side walls with strips of bright patterns and design. The heightened colors reflect the popular palette of the psychedelic sixties and move the windows beyond the somber tradition of church and synagogue stained glass, long dominated by deep primary hues of red and blue, and tied together with the latticework of black lines of lead.

In *The Prophetic Quest* there are plenty of reds and blues—of all shades—but these are punctuated by flecks, streaks, bubbles, and blobs of yellow, green, orange, purple, and pink. On closer look, the lines and colors take form as figures, faces, symbols, and Hebrew and English letters. These are not just abstract and expressive images, but complex designs in which art, scripture, history, and modern life are interwoven. This colorful mix recalls the epic paintings of Jewish history by Hugo Ballin in the Wilshire Boulevard Temple in Los Angeles, created in the 1920s, and demands many viewings in different light. Each KI window and each prophet draws one in; each panel is so rich in imagery and text. It is hard to name a favorite—they change as the light changes and scenes crescendo and fade away.

Landau's windows continue the tradition of stained glass in Reform synagogues that dates to the 1870s, when colored windows with Jewish symbols and inspirational scriptural passages were first installed in synagogues in Cincinnati, Baltimore, New York City, and Charleston, South Carolina. In its color and form, however, and its narrative and symbolic ambition, *The Prophetic Quest* compares with more modern works: Abraham Rattner's grand window at the Chicago Loop Synagogue (1958) and Ben Shahn's massive windows at Temple Beth Zion in Buffalo (1967).

With its mix of old and new imagery, this past and present tie together in the best Jewish tradition. Listen to the Prophets! Their words remain alive today with meaning—as alive as Landau's windows.

The True Line

Scott Knauer

As an artist, educator, and gallery director, what strikes me most as I view the stained glass windows by Jacob Landau is the brilliant dance of color and light as they weave through the complex lines of this beautiful ten-panel piece.

I have always been in awe of Jacob Landau's command of line and form. Whether creating a delicate hairline mark or a bold, dark, and dramatic one, his line is true and meaningful and flows effortlessly across the page. In *The Prophetic Quest*, his eye for color and composition is on majestic display.

In viewing the panels, from one to the next, I can't help but get caught up in the movement of the shapes and colors as they merge so seamlessly throughout the overall composition. *The Prophetic Quest* is a masterwork that will be enjoyed for ages to come.

A Surrealist Poem

John G. McEllhenney

To walk into the sanctuary of Reform Congregation Keneseth Israel is to enter a surrealist poem—not one written in black on white paper, rather one composed of pieces of colored glass. But as with all surrealist poetry, our everyday picture of what is real is shattered, challenging us to use the shards to create a new view of reality.

The color red, so dominant in the windows when viewed from the back of the sanctuary, reveals the blood being let by today's life-destroying drive to be Number One. Red also reveals the passionate protest by today's prophets against the quest for money, power, sex, and fame.

A prophetic image in one window clings to my imagination—the image of Jeremiah, his face lost in blurs of color, running through the streets of any time and any place. His sprinting legs are multicolored, mimicking the pantaloons of Harlequin. He exposes his pink penis and carries a mask with red mouth and cheeks. His eyes drill holes in human souls.

I hear the mask crying out through its eyes: Woe to you who react in pious horror to uncovered genitals, yet are not horrified by naked idolization of winning and wealth, nor mortified by naked indifference to the common good.

The red of passion and blood is the dominant color from the back of the sanctuary. But when the windows are viewed from the ark, looking out across the bimah where the Torah is read, blue dims the red, diminishing its impact. Blue, the color of the heavens, signals a new view of reality. It sings of the ultimate triumph of the Holy One.

Windows into the Mind of God

Jack Miles

One way, perhaps the normal way, to think of Jacob Landau's ten windows is to take each window as a visionary representation of one of the ten prophets. Another way, however, is to think of each window as the Word of God, coming as a different vision each time to each of the prophets named. This way—taking the set as ten windows into the mind of God—might explain why, though each differs somehow from the others, each also somehow resembles the others.

I wrote about this way of understanding prophecy in 1995:

> An alternate path to coherence [in understanding prophecy] is to proceed on the assumption that these messages do all come from the same divine character but then to infer from the contradictions that the character must be in distress. In such a reading, the breach of the covenant, the fall of Jerusalem, and the exile of Israel to Babylon are each seen as a crisis in the life of God as well as in the life of the nation.
>
> Imagine the biographer of God as the biographer of the commanding general in some epochal, ancient war. Having relied on the major surviving history of the war, in which the general may be the central character but is far from the only one, the biographer, by a great stroke of luck, comes into possession of three large and twelve smaller troves of the general's personal correspondence—the fifteen books of prophecy. No simple sense can be made of these letters; and yet, they are a breathtaking discovery, a set of windows into the mind of the commander, into the mind of God. (*God: A Biography*, 195–96, adapted)

Rediscovering Landau

Barry Moser

I discovered Jacob Landau's work when I was in college in Alabama during the late 1950s. It was his *Cinna the Poet* that I first saw—reproduced in a magazine such as *Time* or *Newsweek*. I cut out the tiny reproduction and stashed it away, the first deposit in a file I began keeping about him and his work.

It is now exactly sixty years after that initial encounter. Sixty years that have only intensified my admiration of Landau's work, specifically his graphic work—the woodcuts and lithographs of which he was a master.

And now I look at his stained glass windows for the first time, as an old man, and I am transported. The compositional structures of the work I was first aware of—and have known all these years—are there. Certainly. But then . . . *then*, there's that color. I've never associated color with Landau—*not color like that*! Color that on first encounter diminishes narrative content, ameliorates the travails of the human spirit I associate with him, but which, upon study, gives a new vitalization to his subject matter. Seeing these windows for the first time marks for me a welcome and joyous reacquaintance with the artist. A new way to enjoy, indeed to be enveloped, by the work of an American master who never pandered to the fashionable.

Vision of Light and of Language

Alicia Suskin Ostriker

What are we seeing when we see these windows? Light and language. What do light and language mean? They give us images and words, yes, and beyond the images and words, or before the images and words, what are they? Light and language may reveal the presence of the Divine among us.

Jews have two ways of understanding what we mean by God. In the first, God is like a person, but larger and mightier, to whom we can imagine praying, whom we can imagine loving us, being angry at us, commanding us, fighting on our side, answering our prayers. Hurting and healing. Someone like the giants who were our parents. Everyone has heard of that one, that One. Lord, God, JHWH. Almost all people conceive of that One as a kinglike male being, whether they believe in Him or not, whether they love Him or not, whether they fear Him or not.

Among Jewish mystics, the One is both male and female. The male and female are one. They emerge from that which is without end, *ein sof.* An abstraction, not an image. We can have no image, knowledge, or understanding of this divine holiness, this pinpoint of pure energy pervading the universe, pure impersonal being exploding, as in the big bang of the cosmologists, energy collapsing into matter, or spirit descending into atoms. We can never have any personal relationship with the impersonal One, the boundless One, sheer existence everywhere or nowhere. And yet we invoke hashem, the Name. Baruch hashem, we say. Blessed is the Name.

This is a paradox, but you cannot say anything believable about God without paradox. Light streaming at the limits of velocity. The laws of physics, later the laws of chemistry, light streaming through glass, the riddle of existence. Light that is indifferent to our existence. That is God. Spinoza's God, perhaps. Or the God of the Enlightenment. Yet God is also the One who is intimate with us through language. Using language, that One listens and speaks, commands, blesses, and curses. We human beings have stolen the music of language from God, like Prometheus stealing fire from Zeus. Language tells us who we are, what good and evil are, what we may be, what we may do.

Color is the passion of the visible. Light streaming through colored glass is a glory. Colored glass broken into outlines of people and things is a story. Glory and story is what we see when we look at these windows. The force of the glory, those reds like flame, those blues like midday sky, those fierce greens, those yellows. All passion.

Shapes of bodies, bodies dynamic with energy and action, trees, vines, snakes, bones, fragments framed in windows. Before we read the words we may be overwhelmed by the power of these broken images. Broken yet intense. Stories broken yet still intense, like the Bible stories we half remember, the prophets whose words we are in danger of forgetting. As the images of radiant broken glass in these windows draw transcendence down into our broken world, so the words embedded along the borders of the windows reach from our material lives toward a spirituality of which we can dream. These sentences are among the most provocative utterances on the planet. "Will you indeed destroy the righteous with the wicked?" Abraham asks God, a question that has particular force after the Shoah. "The wolf shall dwell with the lamb," Isaiah promises, and we are moved by a yearning for peace. "Lamentation and bitter weeping," Jeremiah's summation of Jerusalem's fate, might be seen as a summary of Jewish history or indeed of all human history.

The prophets were broken men. The world broke them. But God broke into them and used them as his voice. The prophets bequeathed a language of gloriousness and power, of promise and warning, to the Jews and to all people who aspire in the direction of the light.

Seers and See-ers

Kent Harold Richards

Jacob Landau has reinforced to all "see-ers" of the windows that Abraham and Job have long been a part of a pantheon of prophets, continuing a rich tradition in the three Abrahamic religions. Judaism, Christianity, and Islam have long spoken of Abraham and Job as seers/prophets and highlighted their visionary qualities. This inclusion of Abraham and Job in Landau's *The Prophetic Quest*, even if their names are not listed among the seers/prophets in the Hebrew Bible, can serve as a reminder that the canonical shape of the biblical texts in our religious traditions may, like our human color sensors, blind us or open us to who qualifies as a seer/prophet.

I'm reminded of the Common Bluebottle butterfly, which has fifteen types of photo pigment in its eyes—not just the three we have—and so can see more color than we can. So Landau sees more prophets.

Some may also be color-limited by envisioning only a single Isaiah. But Landau, like the Bluebottle butterfly, sees more and gives us both Isaiah and the Second Isaiah, chronicled in the latter part of the book of Isaiah. Scholars of the "canon," by whatever intellectual or theological tradition, now regard the sixty-six chapters of Isaiah as consisting of at least two parts, if not three. This division of the book of Isaiah is already evident in a Dead Sea Scroll manuscript and certainly has been commonplace since the Enlightenment.

Whenever you view or contemplate the power of these windows as a "see-er," remember that none of us has captured the total light these Landau windows can and will bring us. None of us has attained the stature of Moses in the words of the LORD spoken to Aaron and Miriam:

Hear my words:

When there are prophets among you,
I the Lord make myself known to them in visions;
I speak to them in dreams.
Not so with my servant Moses;
He is entrusted with all my house.
With him I speak face to face—clearly, not in riddles;
And he beholds the form of the Lord . . .

(Numbers 12:6–8 NRSV)

Keneseth Israel Caught Off Guard

Lev Saunders

I remember the first time I noticed the abundant nudity in the windows Jacob Landau created for Keneseth Israel. At twelve years old, I had known the windows for as long as I could remember. They made sense in their extravagance, in their brilliant riot of color. But the nudity caught me off guard—the breasts depicted in Amos and Hosea, the bulge from Jeremiah. Such unorthodox images should have or could have changed everything in terms of my relationship with those windows and my understanding of how they fit into our synagogue life. But they didn't.

The frequent visits to the sanctuary throughout my earlier childhood endowed me with memories of sparkling color and dazzling beams of light, filling the sanctuary and pouring over the plush seats. The content, the stories they told, was a whole other matter. Their fantastical yet modern depictions of the "prophetic quest," with their gradients of mortal to divine, have allowed me to contemplate their meaning for countless hours during many a service. "Why is he holding a gun? Is that a jaguar? Why is there a Soviet flag there?"

I am older now, and the windows continue to confound and amaze me. The nudity, although an easy target for childish humor, only serves to reinforce the underlying biblical themes of the relationships between people, the prophets, and God. Such messages seem just as relevant in today's hectic political climate as they were in the turbulent 1970s, when the windows were commissioned.

A Marvelous Discovery

Judith Schaechter

As a stained glass artist myself, I was truly amazed at how the artist Jacob Landau and his studio collaborator Benoît Gilsoul from the Willet Studio were able to orchestrate a high-intensity palette with so many colors. That's tricky—they can turn into an incoherent mess pretty easily. Everything about these windows, from design to execution, could easily have veered into disaster territory, and yet they manage to look effortless and to convey the very essence of a spiritual journey.

Two things people want from their art (but are afraid to ask) are inspiration and enlightenment. And when I walked into the chapel at Temple Keneseth Israel and saw the Landau prophet windows for the first time, I was speechless. Speechless is a good indication of inspiration and enlightenment, because they are both signaled by a sharp inhalation of breath and excitement, caused by the sudden realization of awe. Awe that one is on the threshold of a marvelous discovery—that beauty still exists in this world and that it can connect us to a "cosmic context," for lack of a better term for the feeling of being "at one." This is the essence of the spiritual function of stained glass.

Radiant, colored light is breathtakingly beautiful and full of the promise of enlightenment. Only rarely does stained glass succeed in fulfilling this promise. But these windows do.

A Sense of Urgency

Lynne Solomon

The monumental stained glass windows *The Prophetic Quest* are a rich, passionate, visionary image to behold. Their glorious vivid color, the complexity and integration of the images, and their compositional arrangement project enormous significance. The messages of the prophets in each window reflect this same sense of power. Their words, together with the formal elements, elicit a potent sense of urgency.

Each window brings us to a state of inquiry. As we contemplate and decipher each window, we find ourselves searching for life's meaning. This was Landau's internal quest as well. We are asked to live worthy lives, devoid of evil, as sincere humanitarians.

Landau was continually examining our troubled existence. Today the windows remain timeless. The ancient stories are presented with contemporary images, images we can relate to today. Time has not changed our issues and concerns. In the final window we see the prophet Malachi, warning of nuclear consequences for our actions. That same window depicts a child leading the way to a new future.

I was mesmerized, as many are, when I first stepped into the sanctuary. I immediately felt that the windows had the capacity to raise my consciousness. Landau acts as a mentor, friend, activist, and philosopher for all who experience his artistic masterpiece.

Painting with Light

Barbara Z. Tortorello

The Jacob Landau stained glass window cycle, *The Prophetic Quest*, is an astonishing marriage of ancient and modern, image and text.

The art and craft of stained glass, painting with light, created in ancient times, reached its zenith in the windows of the great cathedrals of medieval Europe over one thousand years ago. Then, as now, these masterpieces of color and light created a spiritual space and provided a glimpse of heaven on earth.

The Landau windows, with their vibrant, dramatic, pulsating colors and their strong, sometimes jagged, sometimes fluid lines, envelop us in an intellectual and emotional experience. Listen to these colors and see the music of the words of the prophets as the colors, light, lines, and spaces cascade and tumble together, forming an image both abstract and realistic.

We see Abraham, the patriarch, growing out of the serpent-entwined tree in the Garden of Eden. We see Elijah, securely rooted in his unwavering faith in God and in justice. We see the Isaiah window with its images of the Jesse tree, and in the next window, Ezekiel, a central, monumental figure, grieving and yet hopeful as he rises above the skulls and bones of the tragedies to come. The warnings of Hosea, and their dire consequences, swirl through his window in violent reds, oranges, and yellows. Landau uses the same intense oranges and yellows to portray Jeremiah, who warns against the excesses of his age, and yet the artist also gives us hope for redemption with the inclusion of a rainbow at the top of the window. Job transcends his unfathomable misfortune and suffering, surrounded by a comforting blue. This use of blue is mirrored in the Malachi window, with its ultimate message of hope and peace.

We are at first overwhelmed and overawed, but then as we allow the light to reveal the art, these mysterious and awesome shapes, colors, and texts seem to arrange themselves into more comprehensive images, while at the same time transcending our vision and our consciousness.

A Comic Strip in Sacred Space

JT Waldman

What an enlightening concept: a huge comic strip in a sacred space. Upon first viewing the Landau stained glass windows known as *The Prophetic Quest*, I was struck with the graphic nature of the works. The serpentine black metal lines dividing forms of color, the interplay of text and image, and the series of windows related by subject matter are definitive identifiers of the sequential art form.

It was clear to me that Landau had created a stained glass comic strip with word balloons and exaggerated gestures. Despite its monumental scale and religious setting, *The Prophetic Quest* broadcasts roots in illustration and comic books by dividing each window into panels, like a page from the comics. Motion lines behind the figures thrust the forms up and down the windows, while symbols and icons swirl around the windows, shouting to be noticed for their biblical meaning and grandiose themes from the 1960s. My hunch was validated when I discovered later that Landau had a brief stint illustrating none other than *Captain America* in the 1940s.

From 2012 to 2015 I scrutinized, and in some cases retraced, Landau's lines in my effort to create the comic book *Opening the Windows: A Reader's Guide to The Prophetic Quest*. Commemorating the fortieth anniversary of the monumental stained glass windows, the site-specific book is in dialog with the windows. Ensconced in the pews amidst the series of windows, the comic decodes and builds connections for the viewers. By providing context to the blurbs in the windows and relating these ideas to contemporary notions of community and prophecy, the *Reader's Guide* is both a commentary and an invitation to interpretation. It was daunting to translate the intentions of another artist, but I found comfort in bringing Landau's ideas and visions to new generations of viewers. Just like a comic book, which is read alone but enjoyed together, *The Prophetic Quest* brought two illustrators together on a quest to bring communities closer through their engagement with sacred art and spaces.

Window Specifications

Location

The Korn Memorial Sanctuary of Reform Congregation Keneseth Israel, Old York Road and Township Line Road, Elkins Park, Pennsylvania.

Principals

Jacob Landau, artist.

Benoît D. Gilsoul, stained glass artist, translated Landau's drawing into window-sized cartoons, selected the glass, and painted some of the segments.

Willet Stained Glass Studios of Philadelphia fabricated and installed the windows.

Morton H. Lerner, Engineering Consultant and Land Designers of Philadelphia, designed the exterior lighting. McDevitt Electric Inc. of Oakford, Pennsylvania, installed the fixtures.

Scope

Ten leaded, faceted, and laminated stained glass windows for the Sanctuary, five on each side.

Dates

November 5, 1970—Contract signed with Jacob Landau, artist, Roosevelt, New Jersey.

May 24, 1971—Contract signed with Willet Stained Glass Windows Studio of Philadelphia and Benoît D. Gilsoul, artist.

August 24, 1974—Project completed.

Technique

Traditional leading and soldered copper foil technique as well as faceted glass. Some glass "painted" on both sides with mixtures of powdered metallic oxides and ground glass to gain texture and shadings of color.

Materials

Leaded stained glass, including acid-etched flashed glass, silver stain, hand-painted fired glasses, antique glasses, Norman slab glass, and glass from other countries, including England and Germany—all hand-blown.

Saddle bars used for structural support and panel division.

Details

Each window measures 5 × 25 ft.

The windows contain over 3,000 sq. ft. of glass.

Each window weighs 600 lb.

The windows contain 2,500 lb. of metal.

Each window is divided into six equal panels.

Over 100 shades and colors of glass were used, many of which had rarely been used in windows.

Over 30,000 individual pieces of glass were used, each cut by hand.

Cost

Total: $119,350

Dates

First window installed January 1974

Last window installed August 1974

Index of Images

Images include the words, figures, and objects in the windows, but not colors or forms (though hue and contrast as well as relative size and scale are significant). This index is our reading of the images, not Landau's directly, though it is informed by his "Descriptions" and "Prospectus" as well as numerous conversations with the artist. Each image is followed by a location reference: Roman numerals indicate the windows (I, Abraham; II, Elijah; III, Amos; IV, Hosea; V, Isaiah; VI, Jeremiah; VII, Ezekiel; VIII, Second Isaiah; IX, Job; X, Malachi); Arabic numerals indicate the panels (1–6, top to bottom). Bible references by chapter and verse (e.g., Gen 18:23).

Index of Biblical Texts

English text in the word balloons is given first. Hebrew text in a balloon is second, followed by its English translation. The Elijah window has two Hebrew texts. For the translations, Landau used both the *King James Version* (1611) and *The Holy Scriptures* (JPS 1917), though not always verbatim.

Abraham

"Will you indeed destroy the righteous with the wicked?" (Genesis 18:23)

השפט כל-הארץ לא יעשה משפט
"Shall not the Judge of all the earth do justly?" (Genesis 18:25)

Elijah

"I have found you." (1 Kings 21:20)

רעה ובערתי אחריך
"Behold, I will bring evil upon you." (1 Kings 21:21)

קול דממה דקה
"The still, small voice" (1 Kings 19:12)

Amos

"Take away from me the noise of your songs." (Amos 5:23)

ויגל כמים משפט וצדקה כנחל איתן
"Let justice well up as waters, and righteousness as a mighty stream." (Amos 5:24)

Hosea

"I will betroth you to Me forever." (Hosea 2:19, KJV; 2:21, JPS)

וארשתיך לי בצדק ובמשפט ובחסד וברחמים
"I will betroth you unto Me in righteousness and justice, in loving-kindness and in compassion." (Hosea 2:19, KJV; 2:21, JPS)

Isaiah

"The wolf shall dwell with the lamb." (Isaiah 11:6)

ונער קטן נהג בם
"A little child shall lead them." (Isaiah 11:6)

Jeremiah

"Lamentation and bitter weeping" (Jeremiah 31:15)

רחל מבכה על-בניה מאנה להנחם על-בניה כי איננו
"Rachel weeping for her children; she refuses to be comforted." (Jeremiah 31:15)

Ezekiel

"Behold, I will open your graves." (Ezekiel 37:12)

והבאתי אתכם אל-אדמת ישראל
"I will bring you back to the land of Israel." (Ezekiel 37:12)

Second Isaiah

"You are my servant, O Israel." (Isaiah 49:3)

ונתתיך לאור גוים
"I will make you a light unto the nations." (Isaiah 49:6)

Job

"Adorn yourself with grandeur and majesty." (Job 40:10)

ראה כל-גאה, הכניעהו והדך רשעים תחתם
"Look on everyone that is proud, and bring him low; and tread down the wicked in their place." (Job 40:12)

Malachi

"Behold, I will send you Elijah." (Malachi 4:5)

והשיב לב-אבות על-בנים ולב בנים על-אבותם
"He will turn the hearts of fathers to children and the hearts of children to their fathers." (Malachi 4:6)

Chronology: The Life of Jacob Landau

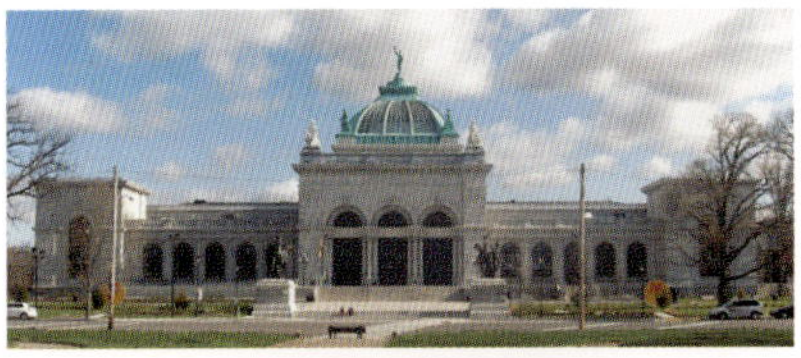

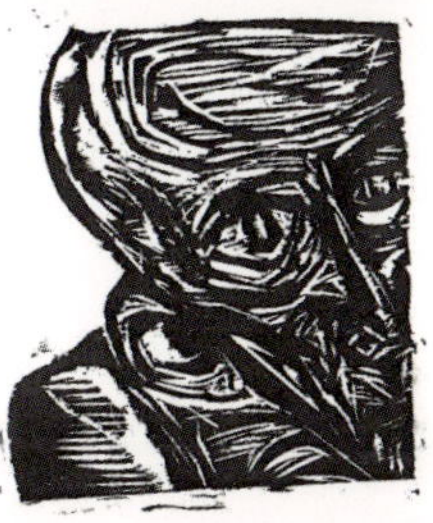

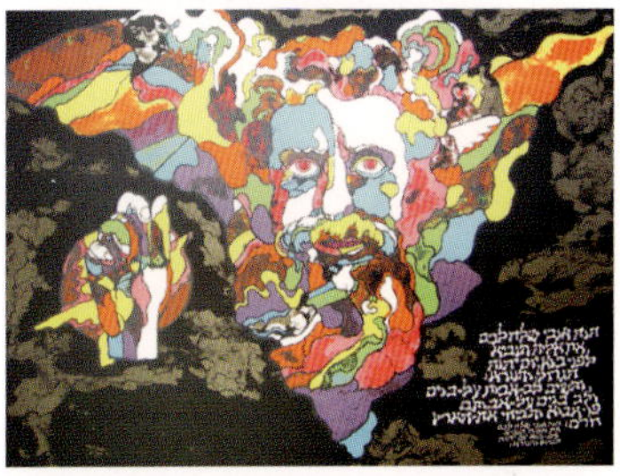

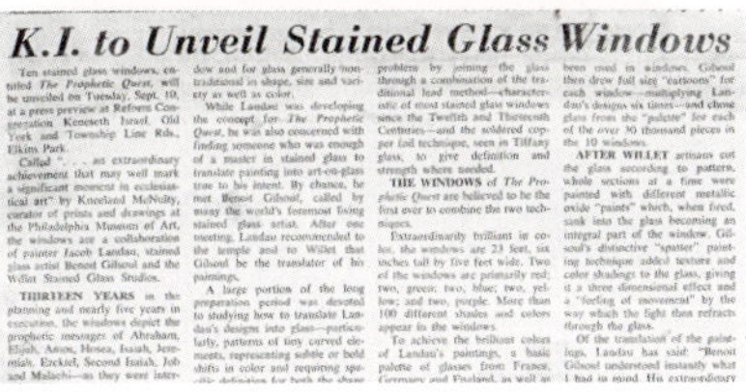

K.I. to Unveil Stained Glass Windows

TOP TO BOTTOM

Memorial Hall, Philadelphia. Photo: Wikimedia Commons (Davidt8).

Jacob Landau, *The Buchenwald Series: 5. Memory.* Woodcut. From the private collection of David S. Herrstrom.

Jacob Landau, *Behold I Will Send You Elijah.* Watercolor. Exhibited at Cober Gallery. Jacob Landau Collection, Monmouth University Galleries. Courtesy of Monmouth University.

Local newspaper announcement of the completed project. With permission of the Archives of Reform Congregation Keneseth Israel and Temple Judea Museum, Elkins Park, Pennsylvania.

1917 Born in Philadelphia, December 17

1932–35 Overbrook High School, Philadelphia, Pennsylvania

1934, 1935 Wins *Scholastic Magazine* graphic arts award, two successive years

1935–38 Studies at School of Industrial Art, Philadelphia Museum, Memorial Hall

1943–46 Army service. Drafted into the Army and serves in Mediterranean theatre (Italy, 1943–45)

1945 Meets survivors of Buchenwald in New York

1948–49 Graduate studies, New School for Social Research, New York

1949 Marries Frances Paul

1949–52 Studies in Paris

1951 *Buchenwald Series* (five woodcuts and one linoleum cut)

1952 First one-person show, Galerie Paul Lebar, Paris

1952–53 Graduate studies, New School for Social Research

1953 First group exhibit, Annual Exhibition, National Academy of Design, New York

1954–57 Teaches at Philadelphia College of Art

1955 Moves to Roosevelt, New Jersey

1957–86 Joins the faculty of Pratt Institute, Brooklyn

1961, 1963 Exhibits at Cober Gallery Shows, New York

1963 Wins Philadelphia Watercolor Prize, The Pennsylvania Academy of Fine Arts Annual Show

1968 *Holocaust Suite* (seven lithographs)

1969 Art for the cover and entire issue of *Ramparts* magazine (October)

1969 *The Kingdom of Dreams Suite*, twenty lithographs illustrating the *Tales of E. T. A. Hoffman* (University of Chicago Press). Watercolor studies exhibited Associated American Artists galleries, New York, 1970. Reviewed in *New York Times*, February 7, 1970

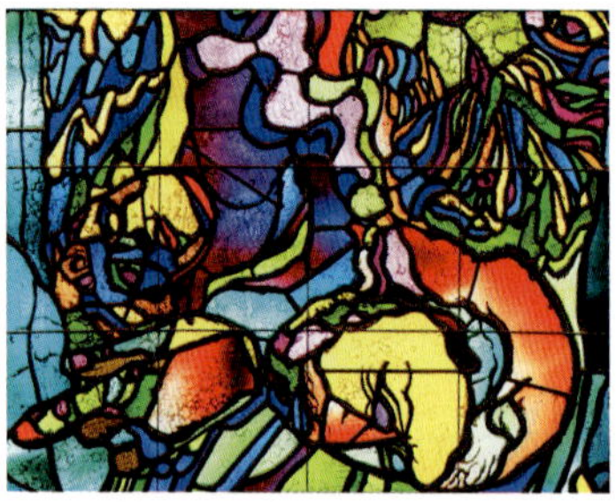

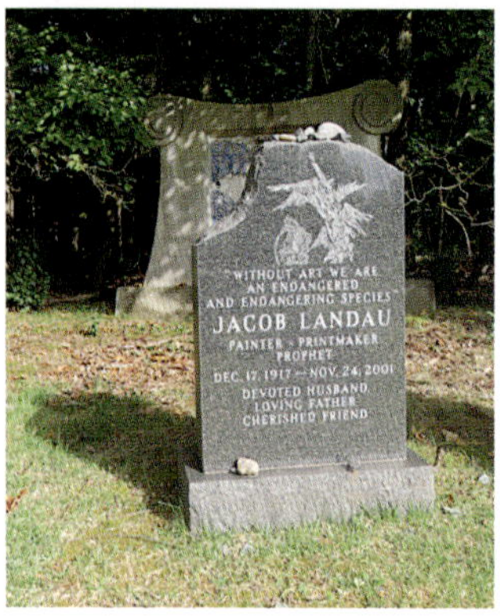

TOP Elijah, window detail (panel 4). Photo © 2013 Tom Crane Photography.

BOTTOM Jacob Landau's gravestone, Roosevelt, New Jersey. Photo courtesy of Tristen Herrstrom.

1970–74 *The Prophetic Quest*, Prophet Windows, Reform Congregation Keneseth Israel, Elkins Park, Pennsylvania

1974–75 *Dante Suite*, seven lithographs illustrating the *Inferno*

1975 Builds geodesic dome studio, Roosevelt, New Jersey

1981 Retrospective of the graphic work, New Jersey State Museum. *Catalogue Raisonné* published 1982

1986 Retires from Pratt Institute; awarded Professor Emeritus status. Serves as Adjunct Professor until 1991

1995 Death of Frances, his wife

1996 *Tree Man* mural for Philadelphia public arts program

1996 Honorary Doctorate in Fine Arts, Monmouth University

1999 Retrospective, *Heroic Obsession: The Graphic Art of Jacob Landau*, Woodmere Art Museum, Philadelphia

2001 Dies November 2, aged 83. Buried in Roosevelt, New Jersey cemetery

2004 Jacob Landau Institute established, http://www.jacoblandau.org/jacoblandauinstitute.html

2008 Jacob Landau Archives established at Drew University, Madison, New Jersey, https://www.drew.edu/library/2019/08/19/jacob-landau-collection/

2008 Jacob Landau Collection established at Monmouth University, West Long Branch, New Jersey

The fullest listing of Landau's exhibits, collection locations, awards, design and illustration commissions, lectures and symposia, publications, etc. for 1935–82 is "Chronology," in *Jacob Landau: The Graphic Work, Catalogue Raisonné* (Trenton: New Jersey State Museum, 1982), 144–54.

Glossary

ark The ark in a synagogue is generally a receptacle, or ornamental closet, which contains a synagogue's Torah scrolls.

aron kodesh The ark in a synagogue holding the Torah scrolls.

bar mitzvah Literally, son of the commandment. A ceremony marking a boy's reaching thirteen, the age of religious maturity.

bat mitzvah Literally, daughter of the commandment. A ceremony marking a girl's reaching thirteen, the age of religious maturity.

bimah An elevated platform, the traditional center of a synagogue from which the Torah is read.

cartoon The full-scale drawing for a window or panel, from which the individual pieces of a stained glass window are sized to be cut. The cartoon is a working drawing showing detail of leading and painting, and is also used as a guide when the window is leaded up.

catalogue raisonné A comprehensive, annotated listing of all the known artworks by an artist either in a particular medium or all media.

confirmation A ceremony for boys and girls tied to the Jewish holiday of Shavuot. It constitutes an individual and group affirmation of commitment to the Jewish people. Confirmation, one of the "youngest" Jewish life-cycle ceremonies, began less than two hundred years ago.

contraries Apparent opposites that are equally true and mutually essential, vital to making any progress in self-understanding, such as "Attraction and Repulsion, Reason and Energy, Love and Hate" (from William Blake's *The Marriage of Heaven and Hell*, plate 3).

faceted glass Stained glass pieces held together with an epoxy, which allows the spaces between them to vary, in contrast to leading's fixed width.

figures, figurative Representation of the human body or its parts.

image Figures, the body and its parts; objects, everything from rocks to trees; as well as word balloons with their English or Hebrew letters.

leading Flexible strips of lead fitted around the individual pieces of stained glass to bind them together and provide support.

lithography A printmaking technique in which the artist draws with a greasy pigment, such as crayon, on a polished slab of fine-grained limestone (or an aluminum plate). After the drawing is fixed, it is rolled with ink. The greasy substance retains the ink for printing, while the blank areas of the stone moistened with water naturally repel it, and after being passed through a lithographic press, the result is an exact replica of the artist's drawing.

midrash A method of biblical interpretation that responds to scripture with parables or even imagined exchanges between biblical characters. Midrash does not attempt to *clarify* scripture so much as to *create* meaning.

panels The six vertical sections of each window defined by the saddle bars.

Pentateuch The first five books of the Hebrew Bible: Genesis, Exodus, Leviticus, Numbers, and Deuteronomy.

prophet Advocate or seer in the Bible who speaks God's truth. The prophet does not predict the future but reveals the present, witnessing injustice and condemning it, saying, as does the Chinese proverb, "If you don't change direction, you might end up where you are headed."

saddle bar A metal bar attached to the inside of a stained glass panel and secured to the window jambs to prevent bulging or sagging, or secondary structural elements set into the window frame and attached to the window panels by solder and copper wires to provide additional bracing and support. In the Landau windows, these metal horizontals secure the window jambs and divide it into six equal sections.

Shabbat In Judaism there is one holiday that occurs every week—the Sabbath. Known in Hebrew as *Shabbat* and in Yiddish as *Shabbos*, this holiday is central to Jewish life.

soldered copper foil Stained glass pieces held together with soldered copper foil, rather than with leading.

Torah God's revelation to Moses at Mt. Sinai. It refers primarily to the Pentateuch, the Five Books of Moses and, by extension, to the whole of the Hebrew Scriptures or Old Testament.

tree of knowledge "Tree of the knowledge of good and evil" in the Garden of Eden (Gen 2:9)

tree of life Source of eternal life in the Garden of Eden (Gen 2:9, 3:22–24), an image common to many religions (e.g., Yggdrasil, the world tree in Norse mythology; Sanatana Dharma, the divine tree in Hinduism)

word balloon A comic book convention, the word balloon is the graphic that includes the English or Hebrew words of biblical quotes, usually with a pointer or small tail indicating the speaker.

Notes

Foreword

1. "Remarks of Governor Thomas H. Kean," Montclair, New Jersey, July 11, 1984, and Trenton, New Jersey, June 6, 1985 and July 17, 1985. Governor Thomas H. Kean Papers, Special Collections & University Archives, Drew University Library, https://www.drew.edu/library/special-collections-archives/special-collections/governor-thomas-h-kean-papers.

Preface

1. The annual meetings of the American Academy of Religion and the Society of Biblical Literature, November 2005.

2. Beth Sholom Congregation, Elkins Park, PA, two blocks south of Keneseth Israel Reform Congregation.

3. Kneeland McNulty, "Jacob Landau," *The Prophetic Quest*, Reform Congregation Keneseth Israel, 1974.

Andrew D. Scrimgeour, "Prophet with a Brush"

The salient written sources on the life of Landau are his "Autobiographical Statement"; Flint, "Jacob Landau," 5–16; Herrstrom, "Jacob Landau: Dialoguing with Humanity"; and Stein, "Old Man Mad About Drawing."

1. *Weekly Reader* was the companion newspaper for grade school students. The Scholastic Art and Writing Awards website states that the contest is "the nation's longest-running and most prestigious recognition program for creative teens in grades 7–12." See https://www.artandwriting.org/who-we-are.

2. During his junior and senior years, when he was sixteen and seventeen. The Scholastic Art and Writing Awards began in 1923. Landau lists the awards in his CV for 1934 and 1935. However, Scholastic lists his awards as 1933 and 1934.

3. Warhol won in 1945. Landau and Warhol are listed as Notable Alumni of the Alliance for Young Artists and Writers, formerly The Scholastic Art and Writing Awards; see https://www.artandwriting.org/who-we-are/timeline.

4. Samuel David Landau (1896–1979), known professionally as Samuel Lev-Landau. He wrote primarily in Yiddish, his poems appearing in Jewish-American publications. His obituary appeared in the *New York Times* on January 9, 1979.

5. The works of 152 artists were included in this 1953 exhibit. Landau was thirty-six.

6. Landau, "Autobiographical Statement," 9.

7. Ibid. Landau called it "a crisis of self-awareness."

8. Ibid.

9. Ibid. He called Fairmount Park his "second home."

10. Memorial Hall, a Beaux-Arts edifice, was built for Philadelphia's Centennial Exhibition of 1876. The Philadelphia Museum of Art was under construction when Landau was in elementary school and opened when he was in the sixth grade. See Noble, "Lifelong Passion."

11. The collection of stained glass in Memorial Hall totaled seventy-two panels and was installed in the ambulatory. Burnam, *Stained Glass Before 1700*, 26.

12. Herrstrom and Boenig, "Conversation with Jacob Landau," 73. See also Noble, "Lifelong Passion."

13. The museum and art school, located in Fairmount Park, were founded in 1876 as the Pennsylvania Museum and School of Industrial Art and housed together in Memorial Hall. In 1949, the museum changed its name to the Philadelphia Museum of Art, and the school became the Philadelphia Museum School of Art. In 1964, the school became independent of the museum and was renamed the Philadelphia College of Art. Landau also turned down a scholarship from the University of Pennsylvania awarded to the student of his high school graduating with the highest grade point average.

14. These included the composers Darius Milhaud and Roger Sessions and the photographer Paul Strand. Landau, "Autobiographical Statement," 10.

15. When he retired in 1986, he was honored with professor emeritus status and continued to teach part-time as an adjunct.

16. Landau, "Necessity of Art in Education," 39.

17. Paone, "Ben Shahn."

18. Roosevelt was originally known as Jersey Homesteads.

19. Somerset Art Association, "Meditations and Probes," 2000 (1997), quoted in *Heroic Obsession*, 8, 14.

20. Stillman, "Jacob Landau," 20.

21. Sarsar, "Transformation." Sarsar is a professor of political science at Monmouth University.

22. The drawing, from 1957, is titled *Baroque Apotheosis*, entry 46 in *Landau, Graphic Work*, 66. Rosa Giletti designed the tombstone with the assistance of David Herrstrom.

23. Landau, "Meditations," 31.

Andrew D. Scrimgeour, "The Windows"

1. Rosenberg, *Reform Congregation Keneseth Israel*, 25.

2. Stained glass windows from the Broad Street Temple have a place of honor in Keneseth Israel's William Fineshriber Lobby.

3. Rosenberg, *Reform Congregation Keneseth Israel*, 25.

4. This was an unexpected decision, for Korn had experience with stained glass windows. He helped design the five outside windows for the Neumann Chapel in the new KI facility. Intended as "teaching windows," they depict Moses, Isaiah, Esther, Hillel, and Robert Moses. They were executed by the Rambusch Studio of New York in 1960, three years after the move to Elkins Park. See ibid., 24.

5. Ruth Schwerin's husband, Louis Schwerin, was the president of the KI board of trustees.

6. Notably, the artist Marc Chagall (1885–1987) was sixty-eight when he began his first major commission in stained glass: the church of Notre-Dame de Toute Grâce, Assy, France.

7. Conversation with Senior Rabbi Lance Sussman, Keneseth Israel, August 24, 2017. Chagall was working on a massive set of mosaic murals, *The Four Seasons*, for the city of Chicago. They were installed in the Chase Tower Plaza and dedicated September 27, 1974. Chagall and Landau were later linked in *Stained Glass* by Lawrence Lee, George Seddon, and Francis Stephen (New York: Crown, 1976), 58, 62, 166–67, 170, 177, 182. The KI windows were cited, along with Chagall's Hadassah Hospital Chapel windows in Israel and five other synagogues, as "outstanding examples of stained glass in twentieth-century synagogues."

8. The work is titled *Let There Be Light*. See https://www.pbs.org/video/geoffrey-baer-tours-chicagos-loop-art-let-there-be-light-by-abraham-rattner. His *Dove of Peace* window for the Flint Institute of Arts in Flint, Michigan, also received high praise and much media attention.

9. Kaufman, "Jacob Landau and *The Prophetic Quest*." Shahn completed several stained glass window commissions, including Temple Beth Zion, Buffalo, New York (1965), and the Menorah Park Jewish Home for the Aged, Beechwood, Ohio (1968). Both were executed by Willet Stained Glass Studios, Philadelphia.

10. Two editions were published by Doubleday and the Union of American Hebrew Congregations Press in 1968. A revised and expanded edition was published in 1999 by UAHC Press, but its cover did not include Landau's Holocaust art.

11. A political and literary magazine, *Ramparts* was published from 1962 to 1975 and was closely associated with the New Left political movement. It was an early platform for opposition to the Vietnam War. Thomas Merton, Susan Sontag, Angela Davis, and Noam Chomsky were some of the authors who appeared in the magazine.

12. Landau, "Jacob Landau: Comments," 3.

13. Friedman, *Martin Buber's Life and Work*, 298.

14. See Buber, *Prophetic Faith*, 193. See also Friedman, "Buber, Martin (1878–1965)," 145, and Friedman, *Martin Buber's Life and Work*, esp. 233–34, 297–98.

15. Levenson, introduction to Buber, *Prophetic Faith*, xxv.

16. Landau, "Notes About the Images Selected."

17. "KI Minutes, September 22, 1971" and "Notes on Meeting with Jacob Landau, 10/14/71," Archives, Keneseth Israel and Temple Judea Museum.

18. From Judges 4:6–7.

19. From 1 Kings 17:1–24 and Isaiah 2:2–4, respectively.

20. Sussman, "Opening the Windows," iii.

21. These were the Temple Beth Zion Synagogue and the Jewish Home for the Aged, projects mentioned above. See https://www.aaa.si.edu/collections/ben-shahn-papers-6935/series-2/box-24-folder-55 and https://thejewishmuseum.org/collection/4943-etrog-lulav-and-menorah. See also Shahn, *Ben Shahn*, 250, 292, 301–4.

22. See http://www.benoitgilsoul.com. Bernarda Bryson Shahn dates this to 1965 in *Ben Shahn*, 354, but the Gilsoul website dates it to 1967.

23. Shahn, *Ben Shahn*, 292.

24. Dove, "Works of This Artist."

25. *Jenkintown Times Chronicle*, "Prophetic Quest"; Battcock, "Elkins Park: Jacob Landau."

26. Herrstrom and Boenig, "Conversation with Jacob Landau," 73.

27. McNulty, epilogue to *The Prophetic Quest*, 21.

28. From the beginning of the window project, the Stained Glass Windows Committee and clergy determined that they would provide an educational publication for the congregation and visitors. They produced a full-color, twenty-eight-page booklet titled *The Prophetic Quest*, with commentary by Rabbi Korn, and placed it in the pews. Later, marking the fortieth anniversary of the windows in 2015, a second booklet, *Opening the Windows*, was produced. It uses a comic-book format to pique the interest of children and youth.

Rita Rosen Poley, "The Unexpected Provenance of *The Prophetic Quest*"

1. From the SGAA website: https://stainedglass.org.

2. From the Benoît Gilsoul website: http://www.benoitgilsoul.com.

3. Ibid.

4. Notes from an interview with the artist at the time of the dedication, 1974. Temple Judea Museum Archives.

5. Various versions of this quote appeared in newspaper articles, including Pheralyn Dove, "Works of This Artist." The quote was in the press kit that KI prepared for the media for the opening of the windows to the public and based on an interview with Landau.

6. Stein, "Old Man Mad About Drawing."

7. Ibid.

8. Ibid.

9. Herrstrom, epigraph, "Dialoguing with Humanity," n.p.

David S. Herrstrom, "*The Prophetic Quest* of Jacob Landau"

1. This impression is reported in Tucker, "Elkins Park Synagog [*sic*] Awaits Stained Glass," 13, and in a letter from Landau to Nicolas Ducrot, January 17, 1977.

2. The rabbi of Keneseth Israel, Bertram W. Korn, was actively involved in the entire project. Landau vetoed Rabbi Korn's strong suggestion early on (1970) that he use a different quotation from Job ("Yea, though He slay me will I trust in Him"). The rabbi thought that the one the artist had selected ("He destroys both the blameless and the wicked") was a "major problem" because it implied that "the universe is really indifferent to man's suffering." Landau ultimately chose an alternative but held his ground, of course, by using "Adorn yourself with grandeur." See Landau, "Notes About the Images Selected"; letter from Rabbi Korn to Jacob Landau, October 20, 1970.
In his "Descriptions" (#1—The Abraham Window) presented to the Stained Glass Windows Committee in late 1970, Landau put a pistol in Abraham's hand, symbolic of the "sacrificing of young men in contemporary times" in Vietnam as a "parallel to the contemplated sacrifice of Isaac." The congregation opposed it, and he replaced the pistol with a dagger by the time he submitted his "Prospectus" (Landau, "Descriptions," 1; Sigal, "Landau's Art Colorful"). Landau eventually moved the pistol to the bottom of the window (see Monmouth University, Landau-MC OU-14; absent in a preliminary drawing, Landau-MC OU-4).

3. Tucker, "Elkins Park Synagog [*sic*] Awaits Stained Glass," 13; Landau, "Jacob Landau: Comments," 3 (where Landau even accuses God of being a "storm trooper"). In his old age, Landau described himself as "not religious" (Stillman, "Jacob Landau," 22). As Lynne Solomon has pointed out, this explains why, in a biblical work of art, Landau ignores or deemphasizes central elements of Judaism, such as Moses, Torah, and Revelation.

4. McNulty quoted in Kremer, "Jacob Landau," 22; see Forman, "Prophecy," 6, for Landau's comment about being a spiritual humanist.

5. Letter from Landau to Nicolas Ducrot, January 17, 1977.

6. Landau, "Autobiographical Statement," 14. "My work," the artist confesses, "has been obsessed by the figure, by the 'human form divine,' in William Blake's term": ibid., 8. Unlike Chagall—and unlike traditional synagogue art, which abides by the commandment "Thou shall make no graven images"—Landau makes the figure central. Rabbi Korn defended this decision, saying that the windows are subjects for interpretation and teaching, not worship (Forman, "Prophecy," 7).

7. Landau, "Meditations," #6. Landau's work, as he said, was "figurative at a time when it was unfashionable to deal with the figure on any terms." But with Ben Shahn, Leonard Baskin, Jack Levine, and Antonio Frasconi, among others, he was "sustained and nourished" by a "strong counter-current." See Landau, "Autobiographical Statement," 10, 12.

8. All Bible quotes are from the King James Version unless otherwise indicated.

9. Between his waves of five windows to the left of the sanctuary (facing the bimah) and five to the right—Abraham–Hosea on the left, Jeremiah–Malachi on the right—Landau reinforced this shift in emphasis from God to man, the movement toward realization of individual responsibility for justice, by placing all word balloons on the left in Amos and on the right in Job, neither of which he does on the other windows. The "sense of feeling of awe" was Landau's "sense of religion," which, he maintained, we cannot live without (see du Cret, "Between Cranberry [*sic*] Station and Prospertown," 27).

10. Landau, "Autobiographical Statement," 9. See the 1935 etchings "Subway" (#5) and *Vendor* (#7) in *The Graphic Work*.

11. Landau, "Autobiographical Statement," 9, 12; *Apocalyptic and Prophetic Works* (n.p.). Landau identified with Hosea, whose encompassing love could only be achieved through self-conquest (2:19). And Buber highlights Jeremiah's coming into awareness of himself as a prophet (20:7).

12. See Landau, "Meditations," 25. Landau's visit with Buchenwald survivors resulted in a series of six woodcuts (1951) that reveal how emotionally affected Landau was by the encounter. (The woodcuts are reproduced in *Graphic Work*, 41–43 [#9].)

13. Landau, "Autobiographical Statement," 10.

14. Ibid., 12.

15. Ibid.

16. Buber, *Prophetic Faith*, 206. In his initial presentation to the Keneseth Israel board of trustees (September 22, 1971), Landau stated that the "general theme" of the windows is the "prophetic message as interpreted in the works of Martin Buber" (Keneseth Israel Archives).

17. Buber, *Prophetic Faith*, 196.

18. Ibid., 188, 191, 194–95.

19. Jung, *Answer to Job*, 534. God's lack of self-awareness and unpredictability explain why Landau felt that the "prophets were basically sad people" and that his windows "had to reflect this sadness." See Landau, "KI: Minutes," September 22, 1971.

20. Quoted in Landau, "Meditations," 17.

21. Jung, *Answer to Job*, 534; Blake, "Marriage," plate 12, and on "contraries" see Landau, "Meditations," 17, 18.

22. Letter from Landau to Walter Kaufmann, ca. January 17, 1977.

23. Letter from Landau to Nicolas Ducrot, January 17, 1977.

24. Landau, "Prospectus"; Landau, "KI: Minutes of Staff Meeting," March 28, 1974. The overall story he announced in his proposal was the "unfolding of the Hebrew prophetic succession," which entailed a

"subordinate theme" (owing to Buber), the "historic struggle to understand the problem of good and evil" as well as recurrent themes announced in the Abraham window: "fathers, sons, the sacrifice, rootedness, fire, the nations" ("Proposed Cycle of Subjects," 1).

25. "For it is Abraham . . . Job's God who replies," Landau, *Apocalyptic and Prophetic Works*, n.p. Hagen Staack, in *Prophetic Voices of the Bible* (a book Landau owned), makes the case for Abraham as "the first of the prophets" (3). Instead of Abraham, Landau could have placed Moses first, as he was, after all, the first and arguably the archetypal prophet, denouncing Pharaoh and foretelling the punishment to come. But Landau chose not to, perhaps because the story of Moses is already told in the ten panels flanking the ark at the front of the synagogue (see Lance Sussman in Waldman, *Opening the Windows*, iii).

26. Letter from Landau to Nicolas Ducrot, January 17, 1977.

27. "KI: Minutes of Staff Meeting," March 28, 1974.

28. This reading of Jeremiah is reinforced as we observe the echoes of his mask-face in the mask he carries and in the skull-like mask in the bottom panel (left side). The normative interpretation is from Rabbi Bertram W. Korn's *The Prophetic Quest*.

29. See Baskind, *Jewish Artists and the Bible*, 4–5, on "creating" meaning; Bruns, "Midrash and Allegory," on the "force" of the text. Landau would have agreed with the painter R. B. Kitaj, who declared that the "meanings of paintings are inexhaustible," as are the sacred texts themselves (Baskind, *Jewish Artists and the Bible*, 139). This is why midrash can be "extravagant, excessive," even verging on the "transgressive" (Bruns, "Midrash and Allegory," 629), as in Landau's Jeremiah and Job windows.

30. Working with stained glass, Landau said, "harked back to the days" when he drew Captain America ("Autobiographical Statement," 14). In addition to using undetermined space and word balloons, Landau occasionally exploits a window's six panels delineated by the saddle bars (e.g., Amos, panels 2–4). For calling my attention to his overall sense of fun, I thank Linda Nesvisky. Landau's word balloons caused the windows committee some concern from the beginning ("KI: Notes on a Meeting with Jacob Landau," October 14, 1971, 3), but he insisted, viewing them as an integral part of the windows' visual-verbal art. Likewise, their English and Hebrew letters form images within the field of the window that question and confirm, limit and extend symbolic images.

31. From the beginning of the project, Landau emphasized to the Keneseth Israel Board of Trustees that the windows combine "architectural beauty" and "teaching usages"; that is, they are "communication" art ("KI: Minutes of Special Meeting," September 22, 1971), a term Landau adopted from Ben Shahn, who called their work "communication paintings" (Shahn, *Ben Shahn*, 15). On the dissonances and his joy in the project, see Landau, "Autobiographical Statement," 14; Landau, "Statement."

32. Connick exhorts the viewer: "give yourself to" the windows as "whole-heartedly as you give yourself to a performance of your favorite symphony" (*Adventures*, 4, 36). Landau follows the Gothic glass masters faithfully, employing their traditional brilliant blues, reds, yellows, and greens. Having never worked in glass before, Landau "felt unhampered by traditional concepts of the impossible in this medium." He "created paintings with a variety [and] subtlety of color rarely brought to stained glass." Also, more pieces of glass were employed in each window and more shapes and colors than in other windows. Benoît Gilsoul, the glass artist, was faced with translating nontraditional "patterns of tiny curved elements, representing subtle or bold shifts in color and requiring specific definition for both the shape and color" (Burbank Associates, press release, 2).

33. On Ratner's Loop Synagogue windows, see Avram Kampf, *Contemporary Synagogue Art*, 256. Kampf summarizes the common "conception of the prayer hall" (239) and analyzes earlier American synagogue stained glass, such as that in Temple B'Nai Aaron in St. Paul, Minnesota (1957); Har Zion Temple in Philadelphia (1951); and the Tree of Life Synagogue in Pittsburgh (1952).

34. Ben Shahn's expressionist Job window was created in collaboration with Benoît Gilsoul, who prepared the cartoons and whom Landau later recruited. American synagogue stained glass dates back to windows created in 1908 for B'nai Abraham Synagogue in Virginia, Minnesota, https://ironrangejewishheritage.org/our-restored-stained-glass-windows; see also Kampf, *Contemporary Synagogue Art*, 260.

35. See Kampf, *Contemporary Synagogue Art*, 26.

36. Ibid., 26–27, 136. The sculptor Seymour Lipton, with whom Landau shared a commitment to humanism, took the path from figurative to expressionist art. Lipton moved from his figurative *Prophet* of 1941 (Elsen, *Lipton*, #8) to an expressionist *Prophet* of 1959 (Elsen, *Lipton*, #55), while still attempting to communicate the "tensions in man as an individual and social being," which he achieved in his later *Prophet*. A striding figure almost eight feet tall, its "phallic spiral" both fuses and drives the "vectored form" that sprouts plant forms from his face and leg, together giving the figure a certain "self-sufficiency," which reminds us of Landau's Isaiah (Elsen, *Lipton*, 21, 33, 46; and see Verderame, *American Sculptor*, 12–13). Lipton's motivation for his later *Prophet* was to make a "self-confidant, challenging human being." And though an abstract figure, he succeeds in creating a "new physiological form of sculptural movement" (Elsen, *Lipton*, 46).

37. Kaplan and Baskin, *Necessary Image*, epigraph. Owing to the great success of Herbert Ferber's *And the bush was not consumed* (1951), mounted on the facade of B'nai Israel Synagogue in Millburn, New Jersey, many regarded expressionist sculpture as the most effective art form for

the synagogue (Goossen, *Ferber*, 48, #66; and see Wong, "Synagogue Art," 37–39, 41). Landau would have disparaged this turning from figurative art to abstract expressionism, his windows being a bold refutation.

38. See the biography of Leonard Baskin, https://www.gseart.com/artist/leonard-baskin/bio. Though boldly figurative, Landau's windows, admittedly given life by distortions and dissonances, belie what he called a "kind of expressionism" ("Autobiographical Statement," 14). And Baskin learned from this approach to expressionism, saying that "Jacob Landau's theory of necessary distortion has buttressed my understanding of form and content" (http://harryally.com/about/quotes/leonard_baskin.html). Baskin and Landau shared a moral framework as well as a "kinship" with Blake and a "preoccupation" with the Book of Job (Hughes, introduction to *Complete Prints*, 18), and both tended to be "oblique" rather than direct with regard to their Jewishness. Yet both were profoundly affected by the Holocaust (Baigell, *Jewish Art in America*, 25). As members of the New York Graphic Workshop, Landau and Baskin published two print portfolios that included their own works: *Negro: U.S.A.: A Graphic History of the Negro People in America*, and *Yes, the People* (see Stein, "Old Man Mad About Drawing").

39. Landau, *Apocalyptic and Prophetic Works*.

40. Herrstrom and Boenig, "Conversation with Jacob Landau," 66.

David S. Herrstrom, "Interpretive Commentary"

1. I am much indebted in this commentary to the late Rabbi Bertram W. Korn for the biblical and historical context of the prophets and for his translation of the Hebrew, as well as to Lynne Solomon for her keen attention to the visual elements of the windows and identification of many of their images—words, figures, and objects.
For Landau meaning is a "pattern among patterns" ("Statement for 60 Square Inches Catalog"). Chaotic to ordered from bottom to top evokes Renaissance paintings of the Last Judgment, such as Dürer's and Michelangelo's. Significantly, Landau replaces hell with earth and heaven with the light of imagination, as does Blake in his "A Vision of the Last Judgement" (and "Job," #14), suggesting that all the action toward justice occurs on a human plane. The Old Testament's world of "spirituality" must be translated, the artist believed, into some "useful form" for the world of human beings. Landau, "A Conversation with Jacob Landau," interview by David Herrstrom and Robert Boenig, *Studia Mystica* 6, no. 4 (Winter 1983): 66.

2. Landau's insistence on back-to-front movement prevailed, for Rabbi Korn had argued that the windows should proceed around the sanctuary because the eye's "natural impulse" would be to move back to front on one side, front to back on the other (Korn, "Letter to Jacob Landau").
My commentary is not intended to be the last word, of course, for as Landau reminded us, "it is possible to interpret the elements" of the windows "in more than one way," saying that even his own comments about intention "should be treated as suggestions for interpretation rather than as road-maps" (Landau, "Prospectus for Cycle of Stained Glass Windows," 1).

3. Landau, *Apocalyptic and Prophetic Works*; Korn, "The Prophetic Quest" (sermon).

4. 2 Kings 2:1.

5. Landau, "Prospectus," 3.

6. Landau had great affection for the bands of the 1960s and 1970s who sang prophetic songs of justice. He quotes their lyrics in his catalog to a major exhibit, *Apocalyptic and Prophetic Works*, such as Jefferson Airplane's "Everything someday will be gone except silence /. . . Seas from clouds will wash off the ashes of violence."

7. In Marc Chagall's *Tree of Jesse* (1960; lithograph), the ancestors sit in the tree branches, which is the tradition of the stained glass windows in medieval cathedrals (e.g., Chartres) and is also sometimes seen in Jewish synagogues. Landau's merging of the body with the tree is radically original.

8. Both Buber (*Prophetic Faith*, 164–65) and Heschel (*The Prophets: An Introduction*, 112–25) agree that in Jeremiah's conversation with an unpredictable and overwhelming God, God participates in the dialog as a person, and that Jeremiah is fully conscious both of his own experience and of God's consciousness of his experience.

9. This tension is evident in the forms piled on the prophet's shoulders, as Rachel, weeping for all lost and suffering children, embraces a man-child (wearing eyeglasses?) who appears to resist her embrace. (In what I suspect is a sly self-portrait as Rachel's child, Landau here, as he launches the *Quest's* second wave, appears to assert that he must find justice within himself, perhaps hoping himself to be one of the just men for whom Jeremiah searches.)

10. The rainbow halo (1–2) is neither Christian nor Jewish, but a Buddhist halo of new conscience and liberation from suffering, such as that of the Gupta Mathura Buddha (fifth to sixth century BCE) (Malraux, *Voices of Silence*, 163, 165). By including this halo, Landau suggests the universal significance of Israel's commitment to justice, Judaism's supreme contribution to humanity.

11. "The prophet becomes the prophecy": Landau, "Descriptions," 4; "Prospectus," 5. On his face is "a beautiful meditative quality," as Landau says ("Descriptions," 4), while his pose and broad shoulders have the air of Egyptian royal sculpture, its strength and authority.

12. Buber, *Prophetic Faith*, 186–87. Ezekiel takes seriously God's address to him as "Son of Man," a phrase uniquely employed by the writer of Ezekiel (ninety-three times), which emphasizes his mortal status not only before God but, more significantly, as an individual human.

13. The hand replaced a static Hebrew word balloon in Landau's preliminary drawing.

14. In his preliminary choice of quotes for the windows, Landau included references to Sophia (Lady Wisdom, Proverbs 1:20–33, 8:3–36), devoting an entire page opposite the texts from Job, which he was considering, to quotes from her, such as "I was from everlasting / I came out of the mouth / of the most high" (Ecclesiasticus 24:3–18; adapted by Landau, "Preliminary Notes on the Prophets"). For her words, the artist consulted a favorite version of the Bible, which he owned (*The Modern Reader's Bible*), that contained both Ecclesiasticus and the Wisdom of Solomon. This book tells how "she came into being" before light itself, sitting by God on his throne and serving as the "artificer of all things" (Wisdom 10:25–27). And Landau was well aware of the consensus of biblical scholarship on the "personification of wisdom" in Job 28 (Murphy, "Wisdom in the OT," 926).

15. This notion implies that the universe is indifferent to man's troubles, a view that Job resists and his four comforters reject, as many do to this day. Rabbi Korn considered Landau's implication in this window that "the universe is really indifferent to man's suffering" to be a "major problem" and wanted an alternative text, a request that Landau rejected (Korn, "Letter to Jacob Landau"). Landau considered the quotes he chose to be "contraries" expressing the "human dilemma" (Landau, "Letter to Rabbi Korn").

16. "God will be more moral as we become more moral" (Landau, "Jacob Landau: Comments," 6). The artist points out that Abraham asks God, "'Will you indeed destroy the righteous with the wicked?' And Job's God replies, 'you, Job, must take up the moral problem, and gain your independence by exercising righteousness and wisdom. You must be my witness on earth as I am yours in Heaven, and bring the mighty down! Power to Humanity!'" (Landau, *Apocalyptic and Prophetic Works*).

17. The artist was aware that his merging of Malachi's head and brilliant headgear strengthened the suggestion of a mushroom cloud (Landau, "Prospectus," 7). This ambiguity reflects Landau's unease about the future and is reinforced by the artist's shifting the word balloon's pointer from the top in an early drawing to the bottom in his window, revealing a shift from Malachi's speaking in the past (promise) to the hand of man speaking in the future (fulfillment). A hand also speaks in the top panel of Hosea, so we see in this change a thematically significant shift from the hand of God to the hand of man.

18. Landau, "Notes About the Images Selected," 3.

19. Job "believes in justice in spite of believing in God, and he believes in God in spite of believing in justice" (Buber, *Prophetic Faith*, 192). The great achievement of the prophets' quest was to separate justice from God. Yet their passionate condemnation of injustice hinged on their conviction of God's involvement in history (Heschel, *The Prophets: An Introduction*, 218).

Alicia Suskin Ostriker, "Introduction: Reflections as Midrash"

1. G. Bruns, "Midrash and Allegory," in *The Literary Guide to the Bible*, ed. F. Kermode and R. Alter (Cambridge, MA: Harvard University Press, 1987), 633.

Bibliography

Writings by Jacob Landau

Landau, Jacob. *Apocalyptic and Prophetic Works, 1967–1976: The Divine Comedy, The Prophetic Quest, The Revelation of St. John*. New York: ACA Galleries, n.d. [Quotes and statements.]

———. "Art in Society—An Artist's Perspective." In *Strategies: A Collection of Major Presentations, from the 32nd Annual NYSATA Conference*, 16–20. Rochester, NY, 1983.

———. "Artist's Statement." In *Jacob Landau: A Retrospective Exhibition of Woodcuts and Lithographs*. Cullowhee: Western Carolina University, 1982.

———. "Autobiographical Statement." In *Heroic Obsession: The Graphic Art of Jacob Landau, April 11–June 27, 1999*. Philadelphia: Woodmere Art Museum, 1999.

———. "A Conversation with Jacob Landau." Interview by David Herrstrom and Robert Boenig. *Studia Mystica* 6, no. 4 (Winter 1983): 64–73.

———. *Curator's Choice*. New Jersey State Council on the Arts Traveling Exhibition, February 1973–March 1974. Trenton: New Jersey State Museum, 1973.

———. "Descriptions of Ten Stained Glass Windows." 1970? Archives of Temple Judea Museum, Elkins Park, PA.

———. "Jacob Landau: Comments." From Landau's notebook, n.d. Box 33, folder 17. Jacob Landau Collection. Drew University, Madison, NJ.

———. *Jacob Landau: The Graphic Work; Catalogue Raisonné*. Trenton: New Jersey State Museum, 1982.

———. Letter to Nicolas Ducrot (Visual Books), January 17, 1977. Private collection of D. S. Herrstrom.

———. Letter to Nicolas Ducrot (Visual Books), January 29, 1977. Private collection of D. S. Herrstrom.

———. Letter to Rachel Gaffney (editor, *ReVision*). *ReVision* 6, no. 1 (Spring 1983): 57–65. [On Blake and Beethoven; response to Joel Funk, "Music and Fourfold Vision."] Private collection of D. S. Herrstrom.

———. Letter to Walter Kaufman, January? 1977. Private collection of D. S. Herrstrom.

———. Letter to Rabbi Korn, October 29, 1970. Archives of Temple Judea Museum, Elkins Park, PA.

———. Letter to Michael W. Schantz (director, Woodmere Museum), May 20, 1997. [On the meaning of "Vision" and "Obsession"; his development 1950s–1970s; the Holocaust portfolio; major sequences (*The Prophetic Quest*, "Kingdom of Dreams," "Dante Cycle," and the "Meditation" group).] Private collection of D. S. Herrstrom.

———. Letter to Barry Schwartz, April 17, 1972. [Response to his book *The New Humanism*.] Jacob Landau Collection. Drew University, Madison, NJ.

———. "Meditations." In *Jacob Landau: The Graphic Work; Catalogue Raisonné*, 17–31. Trenton: New Jersey State Museum, 1982.

———. "The Necessity of Art in Education." *World Futures* 21 (1985): 29–51.

———. "Notes About the Images Selected for Cycle of Windows for Sanctuary, K.I." June 30, 1970. Archives of Temple Judea Museum, Elkins Park, PA.

———. "People Ask 'What Are Your Windows About?'" In *The Prophetic Quest Jacob Landau: Search for Conscience*. Elkins Park, PA: Temple Judea Museum of Keneseth Israel, 1995.

———. "Preliminary Notes on the Prophets." Box 33, folder 15. Jacob Landau Collection. Drew University, Madison, NJ.

———. *The Prophetic Quest: Works on Paper (The K. I. Windows)*. Preface by Seymour Fromer and introduction by David

Sten Herrstrom. Berkeley, CA: Judah L. Magnes Museum, 1993. Catalogue.

———. "Proposed Cycle of Subjects for the Sanctuary Windows, Temple KI." July 1, 1970. Archives of Temple Judea Museum, Elkins Park, PA.

———. "Prospectus for Cycle of Stained Glass Windows Reform Congregation, Keneseth Israel." October? 1971. Archives of Temple Judea Museum, Elkins Park, PA.

———. "Statement for 60 Square Inches Catalog." Box 33, folder 17. Jacob Landau Collection. Drew University, Madison, NJ.

———. Statement: "I Have Been Called a 'Humanist.'" 1985? Private collection of D. S. Herrstrom.

Writings About Jacob Landau

Battcock, Gregory. "Elkins Park: Jacob Landau." *Arts Magazine: Ideas in Contemporary Art*, October 1974, 75.

Bickart, Pamela. "Anatomy of a Commission." 1974? Archives of Temple Judea Museum, Elkins Park, PA.

Brower, Steven. "The Lost Comics of Artist Jacob Landau." *Print*, October 9, 2012. http://www.printmag.com/imprint/the-lost-comics-of-artist-jacob-landau.

Burbank Associates. Press release for Reform Congregation Keneseth Israel. August 13, 1974. Archives of Temple Judea Museum, Elkins Park, PA.

DePastina, Olivia. "Jacob Landau—A Many Faceted Artist." *Sunday Times Advertiser* (Trenton, NJ), October 8, 1967.

Donohoe, Victoria. "Emotion Melds with Narration in Stained Glass." *Philadelphia Inquirer*, March 19, 1995.

———. "Jacob Landau's Triumph Is Stained: Keneseth Israel Unveils Series of Ten Heroic-Size Windows." Archives of Temple Judea Museum, Elkins Park, PA.

Dove, Pheralyn. "The Works of This Artist Are Windows to the Soul." *Philadelphia Inquirer*, March 19, 1995.

Dubrovsky, Gertrude. "Jacob Landau's Prophets and Prophecy." *American Jewish Life*, September 27, 1974.

du Cret, Dudley V. "Between Cranberry [*sic*] Station and Prospertown." *New Jersey Music and Arts* 33, no. 10 (July–August 1978): 24–29.

Edmunds, Allan L. "Introduction." In *Old Man Mad About Drawing: Works on Paper, 1934–1995*. Philadelphia: Brandywine Workshop, 1996. Published in conjunction with an exhibition of the same title, organized by and presented at the Brandywine Workshop Printed Image Gallery, February 9, 1996–April 20, 1996.

Flint, Janet. "Jacob Landau." In *Jacob Landau: The Graphic Work; Catalogue Raisonné*, 5–16. Trenton: New Jersey State Museum, 1982.

Forman, Barbara. *The Prophetic Quest: A Light unto the Nations*. Exhibit at the Temple Judea Museum of Keneseth Israel, November 24, 1994–February 24, 1995. Archives of Temple Judea Museum, Elkins Park, PA.

Forman, Nessa. "A Prophecy Fulfilled in Glass." *Sunday Bulletin*, September 8, 1974.

Herrstrom, David S. "Introduction: The Call of Jacob Landau." In *Jacob Landau: The Prophetic Quest*. Berkeley, CA: Judah L. Magnes Museum, 1993.

———. "Jacob Landau: Dialoguing with Humanity." In *Dialoguing with Humanity—Jacob Landau 1917–2001*. West Long Branch, NJ: Monmouth University. Exhibit at Monmouth University, June 2–22, 2007.

———. "Jacob Landau: Humanist and Visionary." In *Jacob Landau: Humanist and Visionary, 1917–2001*. Published in conjunction with an exhibition of the same title, organized by and presented at the Jewish Heritage Museum of Monmouth County, September 14–October 26, 2008.

Jacobson, Carol. "Jacob Landau Pioneers Artists' Apprentice Program." *Daily Register* (Shrewsbury, NJ), January 8, 1975. [Includes photo of Landau, Gilsoul, and Landau sketch.]

Jenkintown Times Chronicle. "The Prophetic Quest." August 15, 1974.

"K.I. to Unveil Stained Glass Windows." *Philadelphia Jewish Exponent*, August 16, 1974.

Korn, Bertram W. Letter to Jacob Landau, October 20, 1970. Archives of Temple Judea Museum, Elkins Park, PA.

———. *The Prophetic Quest*. [Commentary on KI windows.] Elkins Park, PA: Reform Congregation Keneseth Israel, n.d.

———. "The Prophetic Quest." Sermon, Reform Congregation Keneseth Israel, Yom Kippur, 5735 (September 26, 1974). Archives of Temple Judea Museum, Elkins Park, PA.

———. "The Prophets: Jacob Landau's Images in Glass." *Jewish Monthly*, September 1977, 2–3.

Kremer, Gloria Hayes. "Jacob Landau: Protests and Prophesies." *Inside: The Jewish Exponent Magazine* 1, no. 3 (Winter 1980–81): 20–23.

McNulty, Kneeland. Epilogue to *The Prophetic Quest*. Elkins Park, PA: Keneseth Israel, n.d.

Milton, Peter. Foreword to *Jacob Landau: The Graphic Work; Catalogue Raisonné*, 1–3. Trenton: New Jersey State Museum, 1982.

Nadel, Norman. Draft of Philadelphia Scripps-Howard newspaper article on the KI windows, October 6, 1973. Private collection of D. S. Herrstrom.

Noble, Joseph Veach. "A Lifelong Passion for Sleeping Giants." *New York Times*, April 25, 1976.

Paone, Peter. "Ben Shahn." *Catamaran Literary Reader* 4, no. 1 (Spring 2016): 134–39.

Peskin, Ruth. "Synagogue's Stained-Glass Windows Called '20th-Century Masterpieces.'" *Jewish Times*, 1995, 3, 5.

Philadelphia Jewish Exponent. "Artist Jacob Landau Will Design 10 Stained Glass Windows at KI." November 20, 1970.

Pitz, Henry C. "Jacob Landau." *American Artist* 20, no. 8 (October 1956): 40–44, 58–59.

Prinz, Joachim. "The Prophetic Quest: Commentary." [Book proposal, n.d.] Private collection of D. S. Herrstrom.

Rodman, Selden. *The Insiders: Rejection and Rediscovery of Man in the Arts of Our Time*. Baton Rouge: Louisiana State University Press, 1960. [Page 111, plate 64.]

Schantz, Michael W. Introduction to *Heroic Obsession: The Graphic Art of Jacob Landau*. Philadelphia: Woodmere Art Museum, 1999.

Schwartz, Barry N. *The New Humanism: Art in the Time of Change*. New York: Praeger, 1974.

———. "Statement." [On Landau's "vision"]. Jacob Landau exhibition, University of Connecticut, March 8–April 2, 1971.

———. "The Struggle for a Humanist Alternative." *Counter Currents: The New Humanism*, at Aida Hernandez Gallery (opened March 16, 1974).

———. "Editorial Comment: Tiger of Wrath: Jacob Landau." *Arts in Society: Search for Identity and Purpose* 8, no. 1: 352–357. Edited by Edward Kamarck. Madison, WI: Research Studies and Development in the Arts, University Extension, University of Wisconsin.

Schwerin, Mrs. Louis. "Stained Glass Windows Honored." *Reform Congregation Keneseth Israel Bulletin* 81, no. 13 (March 16, 1977): 1–2.

Sigal, Leslie. "Landau's Art Colorful, Controversial." *Philadelphia Jewish Exponent*. [n.d.]

Snowstead, Joan. "A Visit with Jacob Landau." *Sunday Times Advertiser* (Trenton, NJ), February 22, 1970.

Solomon, Lynne. "Stained Glass Window Docent Training Program." Commentaries (1992). (Reviewed with Jacob Landau.) Archives of Temple Judea Museum, Elkins Park, PA.

———. "Twenty Years Ago Keneseth Israel. . . ." [On the windows]. In *The Prophetic Quest Jacob Landau: Search for Conscience, March 10, 1995–June 9, 1995*. Elkins Park, PA: Temple Judea Museum of Keneseth Israel, 1995.

Sozanski, Edward J. "Humanistic Drawings of an Offbeat Visionary." [Review of exhibit at the Brandywine Workshop; on Jacob Landau and William Blake.] *Philadelphia Inquirer*, March 8, 1996.

Stein, Judith E. "Old Man Mad About Drawing." In *Old Man Mad About Drawing*. Philadelphia: Brandywine Workshop, 1996.

Stillman, Yankl. "Jacob Landau: The Humanizing Force of Art." *Jewish Currents*, September–October 2006, 20–22.

Tucker, Judy. "Elkins Park Synagog [*sic*] Awaits Stained Glass: 124-Year-Old Congregation Orders Windows 13 Years Later." *Evening Bulletin* (Philadelphia), March 18, 1971.

Waldman, JT. *Opening the Windows: A Readers' Guide to "The Prophetic Quest," The Stained Glass Windows of Jacob Landau.* Elkins Park, PA: Temple Judea Museum, 2015.

Wasserman, Burton. "Exhibitions in Sight." 1996. Private collection of D. S. Herrstrom.

———. "Jacob Landau Retrospective at Woodmere." *Art Matters*, April 1999, 12.

Writings Relevant to the Conception and Creation of *The Prophetic Quest*

Baigel, Matthew. *Jewish Art in America: An Introduction*. New York: Rowman & Littlefield, 2006.

Barral i Altet, Xavier. *Stained Glass: Masterpieces of the Modern Era*. London: Thames & Hudson, 2007.

Baskin, Leonard. *The Complete Prints of Leonard Baskin: A Catalogue Raisonné, 1948–1983*. Edited by Alan Fern and Judith O'Sullivan. Boston: Little, Brown, 1984. [Landau owned.]

Baskind, Samantha. *Jewish Artists and the Bible in Twentieth-Century America*. University Park: Penn State University Press, 2014.

Blake, William. "Annotations to Watson." In *Complete Writings*, edited by Geoffrey Keynes. London: Oxford University Press, 1966.

———. *Auguries of Innocence*. Wood engravings by Leonard Baskin. Northampton, MA: Gehenna Press, 1959. [Landau owned.]

———. *Blake's Job: Illustrations of The Book of Job*. Commentary by S. Foster Damon. New York: Dutton, 1969. [Landau owned.]

———. "The Marriage of Heaven and Hell." In *William Blake: The Complete Poems*, edited by Alicia Ostriker. New York: Penguin, 1977. [Landau owned.]

———. "A Vision of the Last Judgement." In *Complete Writings*, edited by Geoffrey Keynes. London: Oxford University Press, 1966.

Blank, Sheldon H. *Prophetic Faith in Isaiah*. Detroit: Wayne State University Press, 1958. [Landau owned.]

Blenkinsopp, Joseph. *A History of Prophecy in Israel*. Revised and enlarged ed. Louisville, KY: Westminster John Knox, 1983, 1996.

Bruns, Gerald L. "Midrash and Allegory: The Beginnings of Scriptural Interpretation." In *The Literary Guide to the Bible*, edited by Robert Alter and Frank Kermode, 625–46. Cambridge, MA: Harvard University Press, 1987.

Buber, Martin. *The Prophetic Faith*. New York: Harper, 1949. [Landau owned.]

Burnam, Renée K. *Stained Glass Before 1700 in the Collection of the Philadelphia Museum of Art*. London: Harvey Miller, 2012.

Connick, Charles J. *Adventures in Light and Color: An Introduction to the Stained Glass Craft*. New York: Random House, 1937. [Landau owned.]

Elderfield, John. *Frankenthaler*. New York: Harry N. Abrams, 1989.

Elsen, Albert. *Seymour Lipton*. New York: Harry N. Abrams, n.d.

Friedman, Maurice. "Buber, Martin (1878–1965)." In *Dictionary of Biblical Interpretation, A–J*, edited by John H. Hayes, 145. Nashville, TN: Abingdon Press, 1999.

———. *Martin Buber's Life and Work: The Middle Years, 1923–1945*. New York: Dutton, 1983.

Getlein, Frank. *Chaim Gross*. New York: Harry N. Abrams, 1974.

Goossen, E. C. *Herbert Ferber*. New York: Abbeville Press, 1981.

Goya, Francisco. *Les Désastres de la Guerre* (Disasters of war). Paris: Éditions du Phaidon, 1937. [Landau owned.]

Heschel, Abraham J. *The Prophets: An Introduction*. New York: Harper, 1962. [Landau owned.]

Hughes, Ted. Introduction to *The Complete Prints of Leonard Baskin: A Catalogue Raisonné, 1948–1983*, edited by Alan Fern and Judith O'Sullivan, 10–23. Boston: Little, Brown, 1984. [Landau owned.]

Jung, C. G. *Answer to Job*. In *The Portable Jung*, edited by Joseph Campbell and translated by R. F. C. Hull. New York: Penguin, 1971. [Landau owned.]

Kampf, Avram. *Contemporary Synagogue Art: Developments in the United States, 1945–1965*. New York: Union of American Synagogue Congregations, 1966.

Kaplan, Sidney, and Leonard Baskin. "The Necessary Image: From the Iconologia of Leonard Baskin." *Massachusetts Review* 5, no. 1 (Fall 1963): 90–112.

Kaufman, Hannah. "Jacob Landau and *The Prophetic Quest*." A presentation to the Retired Executives and Professionals, November 7, 2018, Jenkintown, PA.

"KI: Minutes of Special Meeting of the Board of Trustees." September 22, 1971. Archives of Temple Judea Museum, Elkins Park, PA.

"KI: Minutes of Staff Meeting for [*The Prophetic Quest*]." March 28, 1974. Archives of Temple Judea Museum, Elkins Park, PA.

"KI: Notes on a Meeting with Jacob Landau." October 14, 1971. Archives of Temple Judea Museum, Elkins Park, PA.

Lee, Lawrence, George Sedden, and Francis Stephens. *Stained Glass*. New York: Crown, 1976. [Includes reproduction of the Jeremiah window.]

Levenson, Jon D. "Introduction to the 2016 Edition." Introduction to *Prophetic Faith* by Martin Buber. Princeton: Princeton University Press, 2016.

Leymarie, Jean. *Marc Chagall: The Jerusalem Windows*. New York: George Braziller, 1967.

Malraux, André. *The Metamorphosis of the Gods*. Translated by Stuart Gilbert. New York: Doubleday, 1960. [Landau owned.]

———. *The Voices of Silence*. Translated by Stuart Gilbert. Bollingen Series 24A. Princeton: Princeton University Press, 1953.

Mann, Vivian B., ed. *Jewish Texts on the Visual Arts*. Cambridge: Cambridge University Press, 2000.

The Modern Reader's Bible: Presented in Modern Literary Form. Edited by Richard Moulton. New York: Macmillan, 1970. [Landau owned.]

Murphy, Roland E. "Wisdom in the OT: 5. The Personification of Wisdom." In *The Anchor Bible Dictionary*, edited by David Noel Freedman, 6:926–27. New York: Doubleday, 1992.

Orlinski, Harry M. "The Hebraic Spirit: The Prophetic Movement and Social Justice." In *Ancient Israel*, 122–44. Ithaca: Cornell University Press, 1954.

Ostriker, Alicia. "Job: The Open Book." In *For the Love of God: The Bible as an Open Book*, 120–42. New Brunswick: Rutgers University Press, 2007.

Reichert, Victor E, ed. *Job*. Vol. 11 of *Soncino Books of the Bible*. Hindhead, Surrey: The Soncino Press, 1946.

Rosenberg, Shelley Kapnek. *Reform Congregation Keneseth Israel: 150 Years*. Elkins Park, PA: Reform Congregation Keneseth Israel, 1997.

Sarsar, Saliba. "Transformation." In *Portraits: Poems of the Holy Land*, 51. Cambridge, MA: Ilora Press, 2015.

Shahn, Bernarda Bryson. *Ben Shahn*. New York: Harry N. Abrams, 1972.

Staack, Hagen. *Prophetic Voices of the Bible*. New York: World Publishing, 1968. [Landau owned.]

Sussman, Lance J. "Opening the Windows of Jacob Landau's Prophetic Quest." In *Opening the Windows: A Readers' Guide to "The Prophetic Quest," The Stained Glass Windows of Jacob Landau*, ii–iii. Elkins Park, PA: Reform Congregation Keneseth Israel, 2015.

Verderame, Lori. *An American Sculptor: Seymour Lipton*. New York: Hudson Hills Press, 1999.

Vila-Grau, Joan. *Church of the Sagrada Família: The Stained-Glass Windows*. Translated by Uah Simtrad. Barcelona: Editorial Mediterrània, 2006.

Weis, Helene. "Benoît Gilsoul." *Stained Glass* 80, no. 3 (Fall 1985): 244–49.

Wong, Janay Jadine. "Synagogue Art of the 1950s: A New Context for Abstraction." *Art Journal* 53, no. 4 (Winter 1994): 37–43.

Contributors

Susan Bockius has had a lifelong appreciation of stained glass ever since a chance summer job in the Willet Stained Glass Studio Library in the 1960s. The librarian at Willet, Helene Weis, was a great educator on stained glass, and the firm's president, Crosby Willet, was a generous-spirited national leader in the industry. Bockius was privileged to end her career, which included several decades as a civil servant in the Department of Defense, by working again with Helene and Crosby, this time as a design consultant/sales representative for the firm, now Willet Hauser Architectural Glass, Inc.

Cassie Brand is Curator of Rare Books at Washington University Libraries in St. Louis. She is also a doctoral candidate at Drew University, where she held multiple positions in the library working with special collections. While at Drew, she processed Landau's personal papers and lectured on his oeuvre. Her research focuses on the book as a physical and cultural object. The title of her dissertation is "How Books Became Rare: The History of Special Collections in America, 1880–1940."

Tom Crane, a leading architectural photographer, apprenticed with Ezra Stoller, the "grandfather of architectural photography." Crane moved to Philadelphia in 1971 and began his own practice in architectural and interior photography. In addition to being published in virtually every major shelter magazine, his work has been featured in books such as *Cultural Connections* (1991) and the Roger Moss trilogy, *Historic Houses of Philadelphia* (1998), *Sacred Places of Philadelphia* (2004), and *Historic Landmarks of Philadelphia* (2008).

Arthur J. Dewey is Professor of Theology at Xavier University in Cincinnati. His most recent works include *Inventing the Passion: How the Death of Jesus Was Remembered* (2017) and *Wisdom Notes: Theological Riffs on Life and Living* (2016). For over a dozen years he was a commentator for the NPR station WXVU in Cincinnati. In 1987 he cofounded and continues to offer "Healing Deadly Enemies," a program dealing with the virus of anti-Semitism and the New Testament. He is a fellow of the Jesus Seminar and the publisher of Polebridge Press.

Danna Nolan Fewell is the John Fletcher Hurst Professor of Hebrew Bible at the Theological School of Drew University. In addition to numerous scholarly articles, her published works include *Compromising Redemption: Relating Characters in the Book of Ruth* (nominated for the Jewish Book Award in 1990), *The Children of Israel: Reading the Bible for the Sake of Our Children* (2003), and *Icon of Loss: The Haunting Child of Samuel Bak* (2009). She is the editor of *Reading Between Texts: Intertextuality and the Hebrew Bible* (1992) and *Representing the Irreparable: The Shoah, the Bible, and the Art of Samuel Bak* (2008).

Samuel D. Gruber is an internationally recognized expert on Jewish art, architecture, and the historic preservation of Jewish sites and monuments. He is a leader in the documentation, protection, and preservation of historic Jewish sites worldwide and is an expert in American synagogue architecture. He is author of *American Synagogues: A Century of Architecture and Jewish Community* (2003) and *Synagogues* (1999), as well as numerous published reports and articles. He is Visiting Associate Professor of Jewish Studies at Cornell University and a lecturer in Jewish Studies at Syracuse University.

David S. Herrstrom is an independent scholar and poet who has taught and lectured at Queens College, New York University, Drew University, and Monmouth University as well as the Woodmere Art Museum. His books include *Light as Experience and Imagination from Paleolithic to Roman Times* (2017) and *The Book of Unknowing: A Poet's Response to the Gospel of John* (2012). Jacob Landau contributed drawings to Herrstrom's two poem sequences, *Jonah's Disappearance* (1989) and *Appearing by Daylight* (1994). Herrstrom is a founding member of the Jacob Landau Institute and serves as its president.

Thomas H. Kean served as the forty-eighth governor of New Jersey from 1982 to 1990 and then became president of Drew University (1990–2005). Kean is best known globally for his work as chairman of the National Commission on Terrorist Attacks Upon the United States, widely known as the 9/11 Commission. He is the coauthor, with 9/11 Commission vice chairman Lee H. Hamilton, of *Without Precedent: The Inside Story of the 9/11 Commission* (2006). He is also the author of *The Politics of Inclusion* (1988) and is an avid collector of illustrated Bibles.

Scott Knauer has been the Director of Galleries and Collections at Monmouth University since 2005. Upon earning his MFA at Ohio University, he was appointed assistant director of the New Harmony Gallery of Art, New Harmony, Indiana. He is a working painter. His curatorial interests include contemporary painting, exhibit installation, sculpture, ceramics, photography, graphic design, and illustration.

John G. McEllhenney, a retired pastor and adjunct instructor at Drew University Theological School, is the author of *A Masterwork of Doubting-Belief: R. S. Thomas and His Poetry* (2013) and several books on Methodist history, including *200 Years of United Methodism: An Illustrated History* (1984) and *United Methodism at Forty: Looking Back, Looking Forward* (2008). For several years he was a columnist on religion for the *Philadelphia Inquirer*. He is the cofounder of the RS Thomas and ME Eldridge Society in Aberdaron, Wales. Recently he has turned his research to the life and art of Elsie Eldridge, the first wife of RS Thomas.

Jack Miles is the author of *God in the Qur'an* (2018) and general editor of *The Norton Anthology of World Religions* (2014). His book *God: A Biography* won a Pulitzer Prize in 1996 and has been translated into sixteen languages, including Hebrew and Chinese. A sequel to that book, *Christ: A Crisis in the Life of God*, was reviewed on the front page of the *New York Times Book Review* and led to Miles's being named a MacArthur Fellow in 2002. He is Distinguished Professor Emeritus of English and Religious Studies at the University of California, Irvine.

Barry Moser is an illustrator as well as a printer, painter, printmaker, and designer. He has illustrated and/or designed over three hundred books, including *Moby-Dick* and the *Divine Comedy* of Dante. His edition of *Alice's Adventures in Wonderland* won the National Book Award for design and illustration in 1983. His monumental work on the Pennyroyal Caxton Bible (1999) has been the subject of scores of articles and the subject of a documentary film, *A Thief Among the Angels*. He is currently the Irwin and Pauline Alper Glass Professor of Art at Smith College and serves as Printer to the College.

Alicia Suskin Ostriker is an award-winning poet, critic, and midrashist. She is the author of *For the Love of God: The Bible as an Open Book* (2007), *Dancing at the Devil's Party: Essays on Poetry, Politics and the Erotic* (2000), and *The Nakedness of the Fathers: Biblical Visions and Revisions* (1994) as well as more than ten poetry collections, including *Waiting for the Light* (2017). She is Professor Emerita of English at Rutgers University, and in 2015 she was elected a chancellor of the Academy of American Poets.

Rita Rosen Poley, Director and Curator of the Temple Judea Museum at Keneseth Israel since 1999, was an art education consultant in the Division of Community Services of Gratz College as well as an art education lecturer for fifteen years. She developed and directed ENTOURAGE: Exhibitions, a national company for the travel of art exhibitions to small colleges and museums. A practicing studio artist, she has reviewed grants for the Pennsylvania Council on the Arts.

Kent Harold Richards is Emeritus Executive Director of the Society of Biblical Literature. He is coauthor, with David L. Petersen, of *Interpreting Hebrew Poetry* (1992). He has edited numerous volumes, including *The Bible as Christian Scripture: The Work of Brevard S. Childs* with Christopher R. Seitz (2015), *Transforming Graduate Biblical Education: Ethos and Discipline* with Elisabeth Schüssler Fiorenza

(2010), and *Old Testament Interpretation: Past, Present, and Future; Essays in Honor of Gene M. Tucker* with James Luther Mays and David L. Petersen (1995).

Lev Saunders is a member of Keneseth Israel, where he was confirmed in 2017. He graduated from Cheltenham High School in 2019. He has been to Israel three times and has played the harp for over seven years. Lev is the founder of his own company, Your Favorite Grandson, which provides IT services to older people, and is himself the grandson of Rita Poley (also a contributor to this book).

Judith Schaechter has worked in stained glass for thirty-five years since graduating from Rhode Island School of Design. Her work is collected internationally and is represented in such museums as the Philadelphia Museum of Art, the Victoria and Albert Museum, the Renwick Gallery of the Smithsonian, and the Corning Museum of Glass. Her work was included in the 2002 Whitney Biennial, a collateral exhibition of the Venice Biennale in 2012. In 2013 she was inducted to the American Craft Council College of Fellows.

Andrew D. Scrimgeour, Dean of Libraries Emeritus of Drew University, is the archivist emeritus of the Society of Biblical Literature and the founding archivist of the American Academy of Religion. The author of numerous articles, he is the editor of *Just Call Me Bob: The Wit and Wisdom of Robert W. Funk* (2007) and *The Legacy of Robert W. Funk: Reforming the Scholarly Model* (2018). He is completing a full-length biography of Funk. His short stories and essays have been published in the *New York Times*. He is a founding member and officer of the Jacob Landau Institute.

Lynne Solomon is a fine-art appraiser, educator, consultant, and artist who has helped build many corporate and private art collections. She earned a master's degree in arts and education and is a graduate of the Barnes Foundation. She worked with Jacob Landau in creating a docent training program for *The Prophetic Quest* windows. To mark the twentieth anniversary of the installation of the windows, she curated "Search for Conscience, an exhibit exploring Landau's creative genius."

Lance J. Sussman is the eighth senior rabbi of Reform Congregation Keneseth Israel (2001–). A historian of the American Jewish experience, Rabbi Sussman has taught at Princeton University, SUNY Binghamton, and Rutgers University and is vice-chair of the board of governors of Gratz College. He is the author of numerous books and articles, including *Isaac Leeser and the Making of American Judaism* (1995) and *Sharing Sacred Moments* (1999), and an editor of *New Essays in American Jewish History* (2009). He is also a trustee of the Center for Advanced Judaic Studies at the University of Pennsylvania.

Barbara Z. Tortorello is a guide at the Philadelphia Museum of Art and a docent at the Barnes Foundation. She has a master's degree in the history of art from Hunter College of the City University of New York and has completed her coursework toward a PhD at the Graduate Center of CUNY. Her main areas of interest are early twentieth-century American and late nineteenth-century French art.

JT Waldman is a comic book creator, digital designer, and educator based in Philadelphia. He is best known for his graphic novel *Megillat Esther*, published by the Jewish Publication Society (2005). His collaboration with Harvey Pekar, *Not the Israel My Parents Promised Me* (2012), reached the *New York Times* best-seller list. His *Opening the Windows: A Reader's Guide to "The Prophetic Quest,"* in comic book style, is at every seat in Keneseth Israel's Korn Memorial Sanctuary.